I AM THE PARENT WHO STAYED

Joyfully Parenting Alone

By Nina Farr

First published in Great Britain by Practical Inspiration
Publishing, 2017
© Nina Farr, 2017
The moral rights of the authors have been asserted
ISBN (print): 978-1-78860-012-5
ISBN (ebook): 9781788600118 (Kindle)
ISBN (ebook): 978-1-78860-013-2 (ePub)

Illustrations and cover design by Sim Dagger.

Practical Inspiration
PUBLISHING

Dedicated to Austin, my little sprout,
and Elliot, my baby bean.

To teeny tiddly Pip (still tucked in my tummy).

You made me a mother, and all of this possible.

Acknowledgements

So many people have been instrumental in making my own vision come to life. I'd like to begin by thanking my sons, Austin and Elliot, without whom none of this would have been possible. My parents, Mirren and Nigel Baglin, who have shown me more about how to be a parent than they could possibly know and who were my rock when I needed to be carried again in those early days. My sisters, Zoe and Naomi, who enrich all our lives. Thank you both, too.

My colleagues, friends and supporters would be too numerous to name. But special thanks are owed to Izzy, Rebecca, Yasmine, Shelley and Abi. Your friendship and your families inspire me every day. To Dr. Steve Lake, for showing me that great leadership is compassion in action. Your generosity and understanding when I needed it most gave me the belief that I was worthy when I felt I was not.

To my coaches Simon Bailey, Averil Leimon, Angela Lauria and Helen Henley. Thank you for teaching me how to question myself, stretch myself, respect myself and give myself credit where credit's due. Each one of you has helped me become a stronger person and, in turn, a better coach myself. Simon, special thanks are owed to you for standing with me at my first gateway to coaching, and for guiding me in my first ever vision — I salute you!

Finally, to Pip, who has been gestating along with this book and who will be born just about the same time. Thank you for new beginnings, the gift of second chances and the love you are bringing into all our lives again. We cannot wait to meet you! And to Jim, for helping bring this book and our expanding family to life.

Table of Contents

Introduction: The promise

If you're reading this book, it's a safe bet that you're feeling overwhelmed, unhappy and quite possibly afraid of the next decade of your life. Being a lone parent of children who have experienced a traumatic family breakdown wasn't part of your life plan. In fact, if you even had a life plan, it went up in smoke a while ago.

Right now, it probably feels like you're standing in the trenches, battling to survive each day as a lone parent. Life may seem like one long fight against the feeling that you'll never manage all of this chaos on your own. Taking a peek over the top of that trench to figure out what's on the horizon may just feel too risky to attempt today. Even though you desperately want things to change, it feels like there's safety in sticking to what you know.

If getting through the day with no greater ambition than closing your eyes at night knowing that 'everyone's fed, nobody's dead' sounds familiar. If you're sick of crying with frustration because it all feels so damn unfair. If you're aching for the joy, love and freedom to enjoy parenthood that you once assumed would be yours — take heart.

This book exists because once, not that long ago, I felt just like you do now. My memory of parenting a baby and toddler on my own is peppered with words like 'relentless', 'exhausting' and 'lonely'. I had no road map, no vision for how to build a better future for my children and myself. I barely had the energy to think beyond getting through the day. It was hard, there were a lot of tears (and the babies cried a lot too).

But I had something you probably don't have right now, and I wrote this book so that you could have it too.

Be it serendipity or fate, when my 'plan A' life swan dived off a cliff, I left my home, career and community to become a single parent back in my home town. I ended up living next door to a Leadership Coach, who generously offered to help me figure out what to do next.

This book is the result of my personal journey. Starting with the bare bones of a new kind of life — living in my parents' spare room, jobless, pregnant, with a toddler. I can honestly say when I landed in parenthood alone, I was unprepared and my life felt totally out of control. If you're starting in a similar place, with none of the things that make you 'you' to fall back on, don't panic.

Today, I'm an experienced and qualified Leadership Coach myself. I'm the author of a programme specifically for lone parents who have experienced trauma. It's called 'Family Vision' and it does what it says on the tin: by working your way through the programme, you'll end up with a vision for your future as a family. Now I'm sharing the process in a book — follow the process outlined here and you will find your own unique pathway to happiness as a family as well.

My promise to you is that you can find your way out of the trenches. You will discover you are more than enough. Parenting your children by yourself will change you in profound and wonderful ways, and you will ultimately realize that you are the perfect person to parent your children, just as you are, just as they are. No matter what has brought you to where you are now.

Family Vision is a pathway I've walked, and it has helped hundreds of other parents who, just like you, are moving on from trauma, conflict or domestic abuse. This path is yours for the taking, if you want it.

I'm not going to promise you a perfect family or a 'happily ever after' because this is not a fairy tale. You will have to show up and put some effort into the process I'm sharing in this book. Things won't change by magic, and just reading these pages can't transform your situation — I wish I was a fairy godmother, but I'm not! What I can offer you is the encouragement, experience and confidence of someone who has been where you have been and done what I'm asking you to do.

The only qualities you really need to change your life are an open mind, a willingness to try new things and the capacity to be really honest with yourself about what's happening in your life right now.

Thankfully these things are free. They don't have anything to do with your education, your financial resources, your ethnicity, culture, faith or family background. You can just decide to develop them — right here, right now.

The decision to do something to change the lives of your whole family might just be the bravest, boldest and most powerful thing you ever do.

My wish for you is that you'll find an inner strength and confidence to step into your authority as a parent again.

I also wish you love, friendship and companionship as you take these first brave steps to freedom on your journey to loving lone parenthood. You are not alone and, although it may feel lonely when you set off, there are millions of families just like yours (and just like mine) who deserve to be celebrated, encouraged and loved. You can join our online tribe at www.ninafarr.com

How to use this book

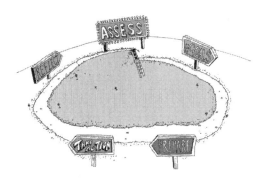

Each chapter of this book represents a single step around a coaching cycle. Part One is all about getting to know yourself better than you ever have before. What does leadership mean to you? What are the foundations of a happy family life, from your own perspective? How will you discover your personal values and how do these impact your lives day to day as a family? Finally, what makes up your individual belief system? How can you change beliefs that disempower you and develop beliefs that support your own growth as well as your children's success? There is much to learn about your jumping-off place. Getting to know where you are starting from is as important as deciding where you want to go. From this new place of self-awareness, you will be able to answer one important question: Where are you starting from?

Part Two expands your inner reflections and takes you on a journey of action, trying new things. The steps in this section are all about making progress, not about perfection. Developing courage while you test out some of the ideas you learned about in Part One. You will be invited to take your first steps toward engaging with your children and the world at large in a new way, driven by self-worth and a renewed belief in your capacity to effect change in your life. At the end of this section, you'll be able to answer a second question: What do you want next?

Part Three is all about consolidation. As you close the loop of the coaching cycle, you will be taken though a final series of steps, designed to celebrate all the progress you've made as you put your new skills into practice. When you come full circle at the finish, you'll be asked one final question: Where are you now?

To help you along this path, there are case studies (stories from clients who have had similar life experiences) as well as examples from my own life and coaching practice. Throughout the book you will find questions you can ask yourself to help you reflect on how you might take each new step in your own life. Don't skip ahead, however tempting it may be! The chapters follow a proven route around the cycle. If you miss out a step, you won't have the foundations in place that you need.

Take your time and go at your own pace. There's no race to the finish line. A coaching cycle is more like a spiral than a circle. Once you complete Part Three, you'll find yourself at the gateway to Part One again. Maybe a year later, you'll want to pick it up and go through the whole process again.

I am not promising you any particular outcome from going on this journey because every parent I know has a unique and wonderful family with their own unique and wonderful path to follow. If we all ended up in the same place, it would be very boring! I do however promise you forward motion. For a parent who feels stuck or sinking, this is a valuable thing indeed.

For anyone parenting alone, this book is a fantastic companion for those days when lone parenting feels lonely. If you would like more companionship than these pages can provide, come and join our community, or consider working one to one or join a live group to work through these steps in person. There are annual retreats, ten-week intensive courses and programmes that span a whole year, a variety of options to suit your budget, free time and learning style.

You can find out all about our group and one-to-one coaching opportunities at www.ninafarr.com

A Note To The Reader

This book is addressed throughout to mothers and the case studies all feature women who have experienced one or a combination of the following: a high-conflict separation or divorce, traumatic family breakdown, domestic violence and abuse. While there are many routes to parenting alone, and I recognize men can and do parent alone full time under similar circumstances, it has been my experience that my clients have been overwhelmingly women. In writing this book for women, I aim to address the specific challenges and experiences shared by women who parent alone in these circumstances. If you have arrived at single parenting through other routes, you may still find much guidance and insight in this book, but you will not find stories that exactly mirror your own. I hope you will look for the similarities and not the differences, so that you too can unlock the hope and possibilities within these pages to support you on your own parenting journey.

Part One

Where Are You Starting From?

The real voyage of discovery consists not in seeking new landscapes,
But in having new eyes.
Marcel Proust

As we enter your first coaching cycle together, we need to take time over the important question: Where are you starting from? When I am coaching, I imagine that I am holding a map for each client so they can see it clearly for themselves. Each one must pick out two points that I cannot identify for them. The first is where they are standing now. The second is where they are aiming for, where they want to be next.

All too often we get excited by the prospect of change and hurry to pick our destination first, neglecting to do the important work of clearly identifying where our starting point is located. If you try and follow a map that has no point 'A', know now that you will get lost as fast and as fully as you would following a map with no point 'B'. It's ok to sit with locating your starting point for some time. It's ok to not know where you are going yet, and it's more than ok to have no idea which path you will end up taking to get there. I had no idea when I unfolded my first map either. Before any of us know anything, we must be a willing student first, accepting there is much to learn.

Begin with the things that you can clearly identify. Who you are being, what you value and what you believe is possible for yourself and your family today. These are big questions. Together they triangulate the first point you will plot on your map: Where are you starting from?

This is soul work that takes time to complete. You may never have taken a personal inventory as thorough as the one I am about to offer you in the coming pages. I am right here with you, holding your map, offering you a compass and supporting your first tentative navigation attempts. You do not have to complete this whole journey in one go. It's enough to take your first step.

Chapter 1

Being kintsugi

....

*'Did you know that pottery can be repaired
with gold?' Kami asked. 'Then it's meant to be
stronger than before, and more beautiful. Which
is awesome, though it seems expensive.'*

*Her grandmother had nodded. 'Makes sense to
me,' she said. 'Why be broken when you can be
gold?'*

Sarah Rees Brennan, *Unmade*

....

There is a dreadful tradition in the West of describing separated families as 'broken'. I have a visceral reaction to the label 'broken family' and sincerely detest the accompanying vision often conjured up by our media. The idea that families without two parents in the home are flawed, damaged or incomplete is hurtful and untrue. The label is infused with guilt and shame. Nothing good is inspired by the phrase.

The Japanese art of kintsugi may not be familiar to you yet. It is an art form in which shattered porcelain items are carefully repaired with seams of gold. The result is both beautiful and practical, highlighting the skill that the repair job has required with lustrous, luminous new seams.

On our journey together I invite you to imagine you are the skilled artist who will repair your family with gold. A kintsugi family is a truly inspiring image. If you feel broken by the experiences your family has been through, take a moment to imagine how wonderful it will feel to repair each crack, seam by seam, with pure gold.

When we lean into the good, we have the power to knit back together all the parts of ourselves we believe to be broken. The resulting work of art is something crafted with immense patience and skill, into something more valuable and more luminous than it was before.

What We Focus On, We Find

If you focus on your fears, you will find more reasons to be afraid. If you focus on abandonment, loneliness and insecurity, you will surely discover these things all around you.

How will you feel when you turn the lens inward instead? Celebrate and honour yourself for being the parent who stayed, and claim back your energy from the parent who left. Lean into the relationships that you have with your children, and remove yourself once and for all from the relationship your ex-partner and you once shared.

When you embark on the journey of becoming the artist who designs your own life, you place yourself firmly at the centre of your own universe, no longer a satellite spinning around somebody else's sun.

Just like the kintsugi artist, you can use a seam of gold to heal your shattered pieces and craft a beautiful life filled with positivity and purpose once more. There is a way to set down your fear, resentment, frustration and anger. It can happen much sooner than you think. This is how it works.

The Problem

Over the years of delivering my unique leadership development programme to lone parents, I've come to a deeper understanding of the specific problems faced by parents who have experienced conflict, trauma or abuse.

Before you can get to work on your own golden restorations, you need to pick up the pieces of your own family and truly understand where the breaks have been. No two families become divided in the same way. But there are common fault lines along which breaks will certainly appear.

Unlike families who amicably separate or parents who are bereaved, those of us who are pitched into parenting alone in the midst of shocking, stressful or frightening circumstances will find deep cracks. These must be carefully restored with love. Some breaks are clean but devastatingly deep. Others leave great spaces that must be filled in with care. Some leave a mosaic of tiny pieces which only patience can restore. Release any expectations you may have about how long this process of restoration should take, or what healing for you and your family will look like. It is my experience that neither the pace nor the route to wholeness can be predicted. As each artist learns her craft, she brings her own expression to the art form. You will express healing in your own way, with your own personality, in the way your family most needs you to.

This book is for you, if you relate to the situations I am about to describe.

Some parents I meet are suffering because of the basic unreliability of their child's other parent. They find themselves unwillingly stuck in a co-parenting relationship with an ex-partner they cannot communicate with at all.

Others are full-time single parents who may suddenly be struggling financially due to missed maintenance payments, a bad financial arrangement at divorce or the financial chaos their separation has brought about. Still more may face climbing out from under debts they have had no part in creating, or be swamped by legal bills they must find the resources to pay for. The pressure of being the main, or only, provider for their family can feel crushing.

There are those who are driven to distraction by the careless attitude of their ex toward stable, supportive contact with their shared children. I've listened too many times to stories about children waiting by windows for a parent who never shows up. To mothers who are manipulated, who continue to be abused or controlled by their ex through the child arrangements they agreed to either via the family courts or in their divorce or separation proceedings.

Then there are the parents whose hearts are shattered by loss, asking with desperation how they can support their children through abject grief after their other parent simply walked out of their life for good.

And there are some for whom their child's other parent is dangerous to be around. Fleeing violence, coercion and control, they hoped to remove the aggressor from their lives and protect their family from further abuse. Yet domestic abuse between parents rarely means the abuser will not be awarded some contact with their child by the courts. This can leave traumatized mothers open to abuse at each handover, and their children vulnerable to further abuse.

Whether your ex is careless, callous, absent or cruel, if you recognize yourself in one of these pictures, I have no doubt that you will relate to the stories my clients have shared with me over the years. Throughout this book, I'll be sharing their words and thoughts with you. I will also share my own story.

Look for the things you have in common with each one. Even if the details are different, you'll find many of the feelings that keep each of us stuck are often the same. The more you understand what's going on for you, the more power you'll have to take action to change it.

CASE STUDY: EMMA'S STORY

Emma was a first-time mum who attended a group programme. She represents so many of the other parents I have met with an abusive ex-partner and co-parent.

When Emma talks about her daughter's contact with her father, a wave of frustration and misery wells up. Hot tears splash down her cheeks as her tightly controlled rage spills out.

'He sees her at the weekends, buys her presents, takes her on treats. She loves going but I am always afraid. Afraid he might hurt her. Afraid of how he will treat me, and afraid that he might not bring her back. It's a living nightmare I have to keep stepping into week after week after week … how will I survive this until she grows up?'

Emma's ex-partner hit her. His violence toward Emma was the reason she ended the relationship, and her desire to protect her 20-month-old daughter is palpable. But as part of their separation the family courts have ordered contact continue with the father. Now the problem for Emma isn't how to leave him, but how to live with him still being part of their lives.

Living your life alongside the perpetual presence of someone you never want to see again has the power to suck out all your hope, joy, optimism and enthusiasm. Parenting with this person can feel soul-destroying. Emma's fears provoke a barrage of questions and, beyond those, some gut-wrenching negative beliefs.

'How can I keep my daughter safe?'

'Am I going to be enough for her?'

'What if something terrible goes wrong?'

'What if I lose her?'

'I feel trapped.'

'My daughter keeps me tied to this absolute nightmare.'

'I will never be able to fix this situation now.'

'I don't even want to be a mother anymore.'

I know it sounds brutal to voice these feelings and fears but, by giving them a voice, we get to listen to the fears and find a way through them. When you say your darkest thoughts out loud, you have taken the first step toward shining a light on them. It is only light that will drive out the darkness, so in this book we will give a voice to all kinds of things you don't usually hear.

Emma's story may sound extreme to those unfamiliar with high-conflict family breakdown. However, unwilling and unhappy child-contact arrangements are a reality faced by thousands of separated families.

If you feel trapped today, afraid today and alone today, know that your situation is not uncommon. Even the most devastating breaks can be repaired, and even the deepest cuts can be healed. It will take courage, patience and trust in yourself to overcome these feelings. I know that you are the best person to do this work, and I am here to guide you, from wherever you may have to begin.

Not all parents who travel through conflict have separated due to domestic violence of course. Your story might be a journey of substance abuse in the family, mental health problems, terrible arguments or a complete loss of trust in each other as co-parents. You may know exactly why you cannot parent or live happily together with your ex, or you may feel utterly confused.

One of the first tasks you will take on as you craft a new, beautiful life is to allow all the breaks that are incomplete to fall apart. Once they fall, your hands will be free to do the work of rebuilding. You cannot keep clinging to something that needs to be allowed to end. It is in letting go that you will find the freedom to move on.

There are countless families today where children move back and forth between two homes, according to varying divisions of time, between parents who do not simply dislike each other. Many openly loathe, distrust and despair of each other. The home you will build for yourself and your children on this journey has no place for hatred, fear or disrespect to linger. The luminous light which will stitch up the fragments of your divided family and make it whole again is simply love. Love which embodies self-respect, respect for others, compassion and joy.

For parents like Emma, attempting to control the influence of their ex can become the sole mission and purpose of their parenting life. They throw themselves into building a case against contact, research methods of limiting access to their child and apply for restraining orders, child-arrangement orders and non-molestation orders. Desperate to protect their precious child from the person they are most afraid of, they funnel all their energy into battling for a victory over a system they feel isn't right. If this has become your story, know that on this journey I will help you to set it down.

It is absolutely necessary to stop fighting and end the cycle of conflict in your family. Because in the middle of this outpouring of energy, you will become unable to see who is suffering the most. Your children, who you so desperately try to protect and who are the motivating force behind all these actions, will live in a warzone indefinitely.

When the conflict continues week after week, year after year, your fear of your children's father will dominate every day of your children's lives, even though they may only see him a fraction of the time. If you left because you were afraid, exhausted or done with bringing up your children around conflict, then it is up to you to make it stop.

If controlling your child's other parent has become akin to a crusade for you, this crusade will take over your life. Although Emma's daughter only saw her father for two afternoons a fortnight, every day with her mother was consumed with the panic and stress of either preparing for, or unwinding from, those visits.

In her desperation and desire to protect her child, Emma had unwittingly cut off the most protective thing her child could possible experience — a loving, present, highly resourced and emotionally balanced mum. Are you the balanced, present, capable parent you want to be today? It's ok to admit that you aren't. That's why this book exists. By the time we are done working together, the parent you dream of being is who you will become. It's closer than you think.

If you are resisting admitting that conflict still dominates your home, ask yourself these questions now.

- Are your attempts to control your ex actually controlling your own and your child's life?
- What power are you giving away by allowing this person so much head space, even when they are no longer around?

- How much of yourself are you giving away to a crusade when you could be giving it to your child instead?

CASE STUDY: CATHERINE'S STORY

As Catherine started to speak, she wrung her hands together anxiously. She struggled to make eye contact with me as she described her son's emotional meltdowns and outbursts at home. At seven years old, he was a force to be reckoned with, nearly big enough to knock Catherine down with his temper.

'I don't know what to do when he's angry. It's so intense, it consumes him and I feel like he's out of control.'

The shame and guilt Catherine felt was tempered by something else which she was struggling to name. Beneath her helplessness in the face of her son's emotions was a fear of his emerging strength.

'What if he's just like his father?' she whispered.

'What if he's going to be the same?'

Pain Is Not The Enemy

In a family where trauma has severed connections, where arguments and anger have seeped into the very walls you all live between, it's hard to maintain perspective. Picking yourself up as a parent again when the conflict is ostensibly 'over' is no easy task. Catherine had lost the capacity in that moment to separate her child from the man who helped to create him. Although she no longer lived with his father, she still saw his father in her son's face.

There is no other connection that will keep you tied to another human being that is as intense and lasting as sharing a child. This little person you created together is indelibly imprinted with both yours and your ex-partner's DNA. You will see your ex in the way your child moves, the way they speak, the way they dance, the way they eat. In a thousand ways their other parent will shine through their being. Just like you do too. There is no escaping the reality that your baby or child or teen is a product of you both. Denying their parentage means denying the truth of who they are and denying them the dignity of being accepted as they are.

Accepting that you will live alongside a piece of your ex-partner can be terribly hard. But for all the ways your family feels broken, know that your child is not one of the broken pieces.

Your child may be processing pain, exploring their own identity and letting off steam in any number of ways. But they are not broken. They are a whole person, just like you, and you can hold space for them to express that person. Their pain will not break you any more than your pain has broken them. Pain will surely shape us, but pain does not have to break us. There is gold to be found in standing alongside another person's pain without minimizing it, fixing it or rejecting it. It is in being present that you can heal their hurt.

When adult relationships dissolve in chaos and stress, children don't simply get over it. Their little bodies are consumed by rage and grief, just like ours. But they have no experience of how to channel it, nowhere to go with the feelings that threaten them to their very core. If the parents they rely on for survival have been scary, unpredictable or have just upped and left them, what can they ever rely on for sure?

If rage and anxiety are washing over your child, your most important job is to be the solid ground beneath their feet. To not only comfort but contain them as the oceans of emotions crash over them. You are the safe harbour they must be able to weigh anchor in, the one who restores healthy boundaries to their world and enables a firm belief that they are once again safe.

I am not going to pretend that becoming a harbour is an easy thing. Catherine felt assaulted by the strength of her son's emotions. But as a result, her son felt abandoned on a sinking ship at sea.

The Journey

Emma was at a crossroads when she decided to take the path this book is offering you. On one side was a path of continued conflict, frustration and anxiety. On the other, a path that led into completely unknown territory.

Emma had no more vision for her future in that moment than you may have for your own right now. Facing years of unhappy connection to her ex, she felt both angry and afraid.

The 'But…' arguments poured out in a landslide.

'But it's my job to protect her.'

'But he's dangerous and no-one is listening.'

'But he doesn't deserve to have her in his life.'

'But it's not fair.'

You know what? Emma is right. It's not fair, it's not right, and it hurts like you wouldn't believe to have to share the child you treasure with the one person you trust the least. Moving through a high-conflict family breakdown and arriving at a place where you are happy and confident parenting alone is not a linear path.

As you navigate your way through high-conflict family breakdown, there will be obstacles and objections that pop up all over the place. Some are going to make you mad, some will make you sad. The path you tread is not for the faint-hearted. Those who walk it are not wrong for feeling outraged, confused, afraid or helpless at times.

If you do feel that way, know this — the truth has the potential to set you free. But it's quite likely to make you angry and upset first. And that's something we need to be clear about from the outset. This book is not going to be a totally comfortable read. I'm not always going to say things you really want to hear.

Sometimes, I am going to make you feel really challenged, even angry at times.

I know people often get angry when they are afraid. I respect that stepping out of your comfort zone takes a lot of courage. If you're prepared to be made uncomfortable, if you are willing to sit with the feelings of anger and uncertainty that are likely to arise on this journey, then you're on your way to claiming the prize that's on offer.

Catherine stood at a crossroads too. One path led her into a search for services to support her son. A hunt for someone, or something, to 'fix' his feelings for him, a solution that would make the frightening force of his anger and hurt subside. A solution that would make her feel safe when she was with him.

On the other path was a challenge set for herself. To become the steadfast rock her little boy was scrambling to cling on to. To develop the authority, kindness, compassion and confidence to hold him and soothe him through his fears and frustrations. Down this path lay the solution that would let her son feel safe when he was with her.

The first path was a road defined by attempts to control and contain him. The second, a path defined by controlling and containing herself in order to allow him the space to unravel — knowing his mother would help him knit himself back together again.

The first path felt motivated by love, but was driven by fear. The second path seemed fearfully hard, but would demonstrate enormous love.

Ending The Warzone At Home

The truth is your job is not only to protect your children, but also to prepare them for the life they are actually living. To give them the skills to be emotionally resilient, the rock-solid self-esteem they need to cope with a less than ideal other parent. To be the safe base they come home to every time something knocks them sideways — and it will, because life isn't about straight lines and happy endings. There are mountains to climb and valleys to traipse through.

Your child will thank you more for holding her hand and loving her as you walk right alongside her, than she will for years of her home being headquarters to a battle plan. No child wants to be drafted into a warzone by a miserable and stressed-out mum.

Your child will be healed when he can lean into your loving and compassionate embrace. No child wants to be abandoned or chastised when his fears and anguish come pouring out.

If you have found yourself in these pages, know this: you don't need to be the panicked, stressed and anxious mother anymore. Each chapter in this book will offer you a chance to take back control of the only person you truly have power over. Yourself. With every fight you step away from, a foundation of real inner strength can be rebuilt.

This book is a manual for reclaiming your life. With each step along its pathway, you'll be given the tools you need to reflect on what's happening for you right now, how it's affecting your life, your children, your opportunities and your emotional world. And with each honest reflection, you'll find another fork in the road. You can step into familiar but frustrating places, or step on to unfamiliar paths that require a leap of faith.

On Faith

Faith, to me, means doing something new, even (and especially) when you don't know what the outcome will be. Faith is a doing word. You can have faith, but to express faith, you have to do something. Love works the same way. You can have love, but if you want to share it, you have to do something that puts it into action.

There's no quick fix here. If you have lost faith in yourself, and you no longer love yourself or your life, I'm afraid I'm here to tell you that that is not going to change unless you do something about it.

The good news is I'm also going to offer you some suggestions that I know have worked for me and for a lot of other parents who once felt the same way as you do. So, if you're willing to take the leap of faith with me, I'll help you build your wings on the way down.

Chapter 2

Overcoming overwhelm

Nurture strength of spirit to shield you in sudden misfortune. But do not distress yourself with dark imaginings. Many fears are born of fatigue and loneliness.

Beyond a wholesome discipline, be gentle with yourself. You are a child of the universe no less than the trees and the stars; you have a right to be here.

And whether or not it is clear to you, no doubt the universe is unfolding as it should.

Max Ehrmann, *Desiderata*

Becoming a lone parent can quite literally turn your life upside down. At the start of my lone parenting journey I felt completely overwhelmed by the changes that heaped one on top of the other. I didn't simply end my relationship. I became the sole carer for a toddler and had a baby on the way. I couldn't continue to live in the home I'd shared with my ex-husband so had to relocate. Because I relocated I had to leave my job. Because I left my job, I had no stable income and couldn't seek work due to my pregnancy, so was unable to rent somewhere new in my own name. Because my extended family could house us in their spare room, I was ineligible for social housing. So, I found myself stuck, searching for an opportunity to put down new roots and start my life again. Knowing it would look absolutely nothing like the one I'd had before.

Luckily, I had the blessing of a family who were able to provide a home for my children and me in the interim period. I am well aware that many other lone parents will not have this luxury, at one extreme finding themselves in temporary or emergency housing, at the other forced to stay in an unhappy house they would rather be able to leave. I can certainly admit that, from my own experience, it was not easy to let go of everything that created the edges of my world. Stepping into a new, undefined version of reality where I had no idea what to expect or who I should be.

Today I call this 'the still and silent place'. It's like a waiting room between one life and the next. It can feel crushingly empty, oppressively lonely, frighteningly dark. However, in this waiting room, this silent place, there is an astonishing opportunity for change.

When all the edges of your world disappear, you can build a completely new one. If you find that leaving your relationship has also stripped away your professional identity, severed friendships, changed your living arrangements or triggered relocation, take a moment to be still. It is in stillness that we can feel the space that has opened up in this place.

Being relentlessly busy helps many parents in transition, at least at first. The busyness masks the fear we have of wide open spaces. It is natural for a mother not to feel safe with her children if she finds herself in a place without shelter, boundaries or safety. I know that asking you to welcome this space may feel like going against your very nature, possibly evoking strong feelings of fear and the urge to run and hide. If you do not feel safe here yet, you are not alone. In embarking on this journey, you have already taken your first step toward discovering places where you may feel secure again. For this new world has safe places too. We simply have to slow down long enough to see them clearly.

Any one of the changes I described above, from separation to relocation, involves setting down part of the identity you once called your own. You may no longer be so-and-so's partner, who lives at X and does Y. Perhaps your social circle suddenly feels upsettingly small. Each of the people who are no longer sharing your life leave a space. A space that can feel intensely painful. Yet from another angle, a space is full of possibility too.

If you are able to, consider the vacancies that have opened up. In time, for each person you say goodbye to, you'll find a space appears where you may make new choices about where, how and with whom to rebuild your life. In each of the 'no's' you hear from others or find you have to say yourself, spaces are opening up ready to receive your new 'yes'.

Even if you have lost only one of the pillars that held up your life, you have entered a new land. You may be living in the same home, sleeping in the same bed, moving in the same circles and yet know that some essential part of yourself will never be the same again. The edges of your world may look the same from the outside, but inside the whole universe you inhabit has tilted on its axis — perhaps leaving you feeling motion sick and unsteady on your feet.

You too are in a still and silent place. For each of us moving into new worlds, releasing old paradigms and unwillingly accepting the new — this space must be allowed to settle. It is hard and scary stuff to take a deep breath when you feel vulnerable or exposed. Take your time and be gentle with yourself while you feel your way back to creating firm foundations and edges for your world in this new era.

It takes time to pick out new hats to replace the ones we've taken off. I didn't become a Leadership Coach immediately after I became a single parent. It took me two years to arrive in the city I now call home. Cementing new friendships also took a lot of time, courage and commitment. It's important to remember, when we make any investment in ourselves, that there is no point giving up on a goal just because it will take time to achieve it. The time is going to pass anyway, of that we can be certain.

Allow yourself to enjoy the space you are in right now. Emptiness and stillness after a big storm can be a truly creative place. When we accept what is, and stop fighting against the inevitable changes in our day-to-day lives or clinging on to a life that no longer serves us or our children's happiness, the space that opens up will cease to frighten us.

Instead of a cavern of loneliness, we begin to see a canvas waiting to receive all the colour of our new life. Think back to five years ago. Where were you then? Now cast your mind back another five years. What about then? Keep going.

Remind yourself often that where you are now is no more permanent than where you were yesterday. If you feel desperate or pessimistic about the way life looks this morning, cast your mind back five years.

Make a mental note of the enormous leaps forward each five-year period represents. You will certainly not be where you are today in five years' time. Nothing is permanent. Not the good, not the bad.

> ### IN YOUR JOURNAL:
> ### MAPPING THE HIGHS AND LOWS
>
> Map your life in five- or seven-year stages. What were the key life events along the way? How much have you achieved and overcome before today? Draw a simple timeline and mark above the line the highs, below the line the lows. Don't obsess — just jot down what comes to mind. Witness for yourself the balance that reveals itself. Notice what you have learned along the way.

Telling Your Story

I'd like you to answer these two questions honestly.

- When you meet people now, how do you introduce yourself?
- When you think about yourself, what kind of language do you use?

Our culture is built on stories. In my experience both as a journalist and as a consumer of media, the stories that make the most impact tend to be negative or shocking. Pick up any magazine or newspaper and it will feature a disproportionate number of stories about some kind of nightmare situation, tragedy or conflict. The same goes for the news on TV or radio. Movies that sell well are often polarized: idealized romances or disaster stories.

When we consume a lot of these stories, it changes the way we think about ourselves and other people. All humans are tribal, which means we feel safe when we are 'in' a group. The default setting of any human, child or adult is to find their tribe and run with them. So, our brains are hardwired to seek out 'people like us' and segregate the mass of the general population we meet into 'us' and 'them'.

Perhaps you had already formed opinions about lone parents, or divorced women. You may have put them into the 'people like them' category. If you had stereotypes in your mind before you became a lone parent, these may contribute to your confusion and sense of identity loss. How will you find your new tribe? If you had negative opinions about the group you now belong to, how will you reconcile moving them to 'people like me' in your mind?

What we identify with matters. As you begin this journey toward a more joyful experience of parenting alone, I encourage you to make a commitment to paying attention to the way you talk about yourself.

What do you say when someone asks you how you are? When others enquire about your children, your home life, your job or your separation? Do you keep everything bottled up inside but have an internal narrative of despair? Or are you vocal about everything going to hell in a handcart, your ex being your nemesis? Do you relive and retell every court date, solicitor's letter, financial woe and tantrum (yours and the kids)?

Do you obsess about the new partner your ex has started seeing, to the point where you hate yourself in comparison or pour energy into ridiculing and insulting them instead?

It's ok to be angry. It's normal, healthy and necessary to have support when you feel overwhelmed. I'm not for a moment suggesting that you switch off the emotions that come with grief and loss.

Just know that the stories you tell about yourself matter. The more times you tell them, the deeper the groove on that record will get. When you pair your new story with the sense that your old life has been swallowed up, taking your identity with it, the story you tell today starts taking on a life of its own. You are quite literally creating a new identity every time you tell your story.

Storytelling is one way we stitch up the seams of our lives. You have the power to tell a story infused with strength, illuminated by love. You also have the power to tell one darkened by hate, weighed down with loss. Recognize that your narrative is a mark of your artistry. Each time you open your mouth to talk about who you are, picture a quill in your hand. Who are you breathing into life? Who are you speaking into reality? Let that person be written in gold, a testament to the journey she has lived.

Who Are You Being?

Parenting alone requires a special kind of leadership. The skills you need to manage a family by yourself are in the same league as those needed by the chief executive officer (CEO) of a business. You're the chief budget holder, the decision maker, the buck stops with you. If you don't do it, it doesn't get done. In this book we will talk about leadership, as well as artistry. The skills, the tools, the mechanics of becoming a visionary leader.

Leadership is the difference between setting your course and following someone else's. Leadership inspires others to follow you, work with you, build with you and campaign for you. Becoming the leader of your family today means taking ownership of your family culture. Creating something purposeful, something living, something dynamic. As an artist, you can create beauty. As a leader, you will inspire belonging, allegiance and pride. If your family has travelled through trauma and loss, you will want to be able to inspire a sense of belonging as well as pride in your children. You will want to do this just as much, if not more, than you desire to tenderly heal the visible cracks your family has endured.

My first question for you as you enter the coaching cycle is:

- Who are you being today?

Who you are being means how you are showing up for yourself and your children. Are you giving everything your best shot? Are you taking on the challenge of learning what you need to learn in order to thrive? Are you giving your children the best of you, or just what's left of you after you pour energy into feeling hard done by, let down and alone?

Self-pity is the first obstacle for many of us to overcome. You will make no progress at all if you fall into the trap of resentment. While you consider what it means to reflect on who you are being, let's take a look at some of the unhelpful resentments lone parents come up against. There is no shame in thinking these thoughts. Only know they hold you back from the life you deserve, and could be enjoying — I want happiness and lightness for you, no place for shame or blame.

'It's Not My Job'

There are some aspects of parenting alone that feel very unfair. In my case, being self-employed and a sole carer means not having a second parent to take over on days when my children are sick. It means juggling childcare and my career in such a way that it often feels like I'm selling one of those two short. It means the full whammy of poo explosions, vomit bugs, hospital trips, associated worry, exhaustion and grey hair belong to me!

The financial burden of parenting by yourself is also very real. If your ex-partner pays child maintenance, it's quite likely that this does not cover all the real costs of running a family home. If they do not pay maintenance, then you will find you're solely responsible for meeting all your bills and expenses.

'It's not my job' can creep up on you. It can creep up in the form of resentment, bitterness, neediness. You may even develop a sense of entitlement toward others helping you. The lone parent who allows themselves to identify strongly with a victim identity — 'poor me', 'it's not fair', 'I didn't deserve this' — may find over time that this resentment sucks away at their ability to act on their own behalf. Leadership is completely incompatible with 'poor me'. No-one can inspire, guide or develop other people at the same time as abdicating responsibility for themselves.

CASE STUDY: LUCY'S STORY

Lucy came to a group I was delivering, a lone parent of a boy aged four. She was consumed with trying to make a decision between two men she could possibly date. One was kind, but poor. One was dull, but rich. In Lucy's mind, she was making a decision about who might one day raise her son with her. She was convinced that her potential partner's income should be a deciding factor in who to date.

As a group, we asked Lucy questions about her feelings. Who was she most attracted to? With which of the two men did she envisage an exciting and stimulating future? Who made her feel safe and loved? Each time Lucy deflected back to her son's needs.

Ultimately the most important question Lucy needed to be asked was 'Whose job is it to provide for your son?' Do either of these men have any responsibility to provide for your son's

---

future? What would happen if you rely on either of them, and the relationship fails in the future?

Lucy's power and freedom lay in accepting full responsibility for her son's financial security. It was her job, and hers alone, to ensure that she and her son were provided for. If Lucy could simply take the situation as it was, and set aside any feelings about what her son's father 'should' have done, she would finally be able to accept responsibility for being the sole provider for her son.

The fact that her son's own father had failed to support them did not mean it was not Lucy's job to do it now. And it certainly didn't make it another man's job to fulfil that role.

She might meet someone who wanted to partner her equally in parenting her son in the future, but she was not interviewing for the position of 'provider' when she dated. That sense of entitlement and expectation was both dangerous and unfair. Following through with this logic, Lucy was preparing to jump into a committed relationship that would be emotionally or otherwise unfulfilling — or at worst, might turn out to be abusive. In planning to become financially dependent on her next partner, Lucy was creating a situation which would trap both her and her son in a relationship with another man who might also let them down. At what cost comes the desire to share the load?

Having her own income would release Lucy from making economic decisions about whom she dated. She would have more freedom to leave a relationship in the future if it didn't work out. Not to mention more freedom to pursue a relationship in the here and now, on her own terms.

Moreover, Lucy would be teaching her son how to take responsibility for himself, setting a good example of how to respect the independence and autonomy of women, and how to have integrity.

It's hard to take responsibility for our own lives. It's even harder to be solely responsible for a child, or multiple children. If you have never had to carry this much responsibility before, I know that it can be scary. When we cast around for someone else to lighten the load, we draw in people who ultimately make more work for us.

Relationships built on expectation and obligation are hard work and fraught with resentments. We attract the same energy we put out into the world.

It may feel uncomfortable to sit with an awareness of resentment, anger and disappointment. The questions in this book are here to serve you. To hold space for gentle reflection. I make no judgement on how you might reply.

In the peace and stillness of your own still and quiet place, try to allow the truthful answers to arise. They are only serving you, and need not be shared. In reflecting on who we are being, it is important to recognize if we are projecting entitlement, neediness or fear into the places where we may be looking for love.

The first step along your journey toward a new family vision is this: commit to taking an honest appraisal of who you are being today. Where are you are starting from? You cannot step forward without recognizing the ground beneath your feet. Carrying resentment forward will only create weight and resistance that you no longer need to carry.

If you have recognized yourself in this chapter, you may now know that resentment has kept you company so far. Trust and believe that you can set this burden down right now and leave it in this place. Each further step you take along this path will leave that resentment behind you. It belongs to an old story of your life. Your new story does not need it any more.

Know that you are whole and complete by yourself. You do not need another man or your friends or community to carry you, even if their temporary assistance is welcome.

As you journey into a new world, leaving behind this still and silent place, walking away from the conflict and stress of your past, you will learn how to call in help from a place of strength. Taking responsibility for yourself is not a lonely path. It will be filled with people who volunteer to walk alongside you and share your adventures. In fact, it is my experience that many, many more friends and fellow travellers show up when you invite them to walk with you instead of asking them to carry you to where you want to go.

Making a deliberate choice about who you are being represents the single most important step you will take into leadership of your family.

Closing The Gap

Transitioning from a two-parent family into a one-parent family inevitably means that, initially at least, you will sense a gap. Even if your ex was cruel, unreliable or emotionally detached, they will have taken up space in your life. It is essential that you find a way to close that gap yourself, before you begin a new relationship.

'I Can't'

The second story I hear lone parents tell themselves, a story that steals more joy and hope and possibility than any other, is 'I can't'.

In the search for your new tribe, you will likely go through many variations of seeking people like you. If you're lucky, you'll have fabulous role models around you who inspire you to achieve more. If you don't, or you are simply isolated and afraid, then your brain will play a trick on you, designed to keep you safe.

Your brain will tell you, you can't. You can't work full time. You can't be a stay-at-home mum. You can't manage financially. You can't fit in exercise. You can't have a new relationship. You can't travel. You can't go back to university. You can't take a risk.

Because people like you don't do things like that. There is no such thing as 'people like you' when what this really means is 'people who are limited'.

Whatever you imagine you cannot do because you are a lone parent is simply not true. I'm here to tell you that you can.

People like you do incredible things. People like you achieve amazing, mind-boggling success. People like you exist all over the globe and they are doing stuff you have barely begun to imagine yet! It's a whole exciting world out there — since the edges of your world just collapsed, let's take a moment to imagine where your new edges might appear.

Chapter 4 of this book is dedicated to exploring why we create limiting beliefs about ourselves, the world and other people that do not serve us, and how to challenge them. But for now, I want to tell you another story, about a mum like you, who can.

CASE STUDY: SEEMA'S STORY

When I met Seema she was living a dual life. On the one hand, she was the successful CEO of a large business. She worked incredibly hard and was well respected in her field. On the other hand, she was raising her eight-year-old daughter, entirely by herself. Having experienced domestic violence during her pregnancy and for the first year of her daughter's life, Seema had fled into a refuge. She had truly lost the edges of her world in that period of her life.

With little more than clothes on her back, some basics for her baby and a steely determination, Seema had climbed back out of the hole she had found herself in and rocketed to professional success. But she was plagued with self-doubt at home. She felt she wasn't present enough for her daughter. She had a finely tuned flash point and

---

was frequently explosively angry, or tired and irritable. Her guilt and shame around what had happened to her kept her locked into an intensely private world. She would not contemplate dating. She was struggling to share the kind of joyful intimacy she had hoped her family would enjoy.

Seema was trapped in the story she was telling herself about what it took to be successful. She wouldn't allow herself to relax, reduce her hours or take more time to rest. She was afraid that others would judge her for not managing to put in a sixty-hour working week, and equally afraid that her daughter resented her because of the number of hours she did work.

Seema wasn't being who she wanted to be either at home or at work. Together we took stock of the situation and she was rigorously honest about what was working and what wasn't. This willingness to be absolutely truthful with herself put Seema back into the driving seat of her life. It was in telling the truth about who she was being that she saw the first opportunities to make changes appear. She found the ability to make a choice about who she was being.

One by one Seema started to answer all her 'I can't' thoughts with 'I can'. I can't take time off, became I can leave the office one evening a week in time for the school run. I can't pander to my daughter when I have so much to do, became I can make time for my daughter so that she is happier, calmer, more connected and secure. Which freed up more time for Seema to be calm, happy, connected and secure — both at work and home.

'I can't' is a lie. Together we can stop colluding in telling it to ourselves, and each other. Lone parents can.

IN YOUR JOURNAL:
SEEKING BALANCE

Use these questions to take stock of your own reality today. Commit to absolute honesty about what *is*. Release all your expectations and resentments when you answer these questions in your journal. Remember this isn't for my benefit — it's for yours! You are the only person you need to tell the truth to today.

What do you believe are the most important things a parent should be good at?

- First list as many qualities as you can think of (consider things like listening, being respectful, showing affection, having good boundaries and taking good care of yourself).

- Think about which ones mean the most to you as a mum.

- Record the eight qualities you would like to track your own progress with. What is most important to you as a parent?

- When you look at these qualities, reflect on how you think you are doing in each area today.

- Now rank yourself out of ten for each of your priority areas, where zero is the worst it can possibly be and ten is the best it can possibly be.

- Bear in mind that the middle ground, five, is a good place to start from each time. Are you performing below average or above average in this area?

Resist the temptation to score yourself as either brilliant or dreadful across the board. Most people will be doing about average in most areas, have a couple of skills they excel in, and a couple they need to pay attention to. When you have identified the area or two areas that need the most attention, break each one down again into about six to eight areas.

Think about the following related issues.

- How is your lack of skill in this area affecting your life?
- Who else is it affecting?
- Does it cause a problem at specific times of day, for example, the school run, dinner time or bedtime?
- Does this problem affect you at work or home, or both?
- Is this only a parenting issue, or something you struggle with in all your relationships?
- What would help you overcome it, for example, education or other resources?
- Is this a practical problem or is it a feeling?

If you're not sure whether your difficulty is practical or emotional, consider these examples.

- 'I cannot pay for breakfast club' is a practical issue. 'I feel anxious about the childcare I use' is an emotional issue.

- 'I do not have suitable interview clothes' is a practical issue. 'I feel ridiculous and unattractive when I have to dress to impress' is an emotional issue.
- 'I struggle to say no when I'm put on the spot' is a practical issue you can solve with practice. 'I am unable to set boundaries with anyone' is an emotional issue of self-worth.

The way you feel about a problem is almost always a good indicator of where to start. When you feel capable of solving something, you are much more likely to try. If you feel incapable of taking any action at all, start by examining the story you have been telling about your own worth. Hold the image in your mind of the Family Vision journey. You are becoming an artist today. Pick up your quill, paint a new picture with gold. Remind yourself unequivocally that *you are enough*.

Allowing yourself the compassionate gift of high self-esteem and confidence is not optional for any parent who loves their life today. No-one is perfect. No family is flawless. You are doing the best you can with what you have, and over time your best will get better. All you have to do today is like yourself enough to begin investing in your own happiness.

Chapter 3

Standing for something

I love you right up to the moon ... and back.
Sam McBratney, *Guess How Much I Love You*

If you've ever looked around you and wondered where other people get their confidence from, you're not alone.

In all the years I've been working with newly lone parents, I've noticed something many have in common. Something I believe is amplified when your road to parenting alone has involved trauma.

We have often lost sight of what makes us 'us'.

A controlling or dominating partner may have ground down your sense of self over a long period of time. Perhaps you deferred to his judgement so much you've forgotten what you like to wear, eat or do with your free time.

Perhaps it was too risky to voice your own opinion in an abusive relationship so you've learned to simply set your opinions aside, and now you're struggling to reconnect with them.

Maybe finding out about your ex's affair, or debt, addiction or some other deep betrayal shocked you so profoundly that you are no longer able to trust that your own judgement is sound.

Exiting a traumatic experience can leave some people feeling blank inside. In order to cope with the emotions of the awful thing, which was too over-whelming as it was happening, the human brain can develop the ability to take a mental sidestep and effectively distance itself from the pain we are truly feeling.

Whatever your road to parenting alone, if it was shocking, traumatic, either abrupt or agonizingly slow, expected or out of the blue — you probably feel out of touch with the 'real' you. Knowing your-self inside out and feeling 100% confident and at ease again may feel unrealistic or out of reach today. However, the purpose of this chapter is to get you back in touch with yourself, quicker than you think is possible.

Celestial Navigation

Each of us has a set of values that dictates how we feel about our lives. When we are in alignment with these values, we feel a sense of ease and comfort. We are able to travel faster toward our desired goals. Our relationships feel comfortable, relaxed, intimate and satisfying.

Out of alignment, however, we feel ground down, weighed down, stuck and heavy. The weight of the world is on our shoulders and progress feels painful or slow. We are plagued with anxiety and indecision and our relationships feel disconnected, full of resentment. In short, we are miserable and can become depressed.

However, even out of alignment with our values, we can achieve objective measures of success. Just because you hate your job doesn't mean you're bad at it. And even if you're not enjoying being a parent right now, this doesn't mean you're screwing it up. You could be doing a great job of holding everything together — clean house, healthy children, good job.

But if you don't feel good about your life, it's a sure sign that one of your major values is being ignored or sidelined in favour of a 'should'.

'Should' decisions are the ones we make based on other people's values. They represent all the times we haven't listened to our own intuition, or haven't trusted our own judgement enough to stand up for what we think is right. It takes courage to make a stand. But by taking a stand we are also gifted with courage.

The relief and comfort of knowing that you just did the right thing for yourself instantly makes the next decision easier. Discovering your own personal values is like learning to navigate by the stars.

When you first take a look at the night sky, it's an overwhelming starscape. To an untrained eye, there is no map. But for a skilled navigator, the night sky is a beloved and reliable source of direction. By pinpointing the most important points in the sky, a navigator can easily correct their course at any given time.

Your values are the stars you will learn to navigate by. Not a destination in and of themselves, but a principle in line with which you correct your course. We don't arrive at 'kindness' one day, but we can choose the kind direction at any time. We won't reach an end point labelled 'bravery' but we can choose to step bravely forward when we face a new challenge.

My values are kindness, bravery, adventure and fun. These four celestial points determine my decisions as a parent, a professional and a person. If I'm being treated unkindly, or putting others through unkind experiences, I'm out of alignment. I feel sludgy and bad. If I'm overly cautious, or timid or playing small, and I limit my life and the lives of those I love because I'm not being brave, my energy is sapped from everything I do. When I'm presented with a new adventure, it fills me with excitement and my energy is conversely topped up. If I find myself not having fun, I swiftly begin to feel trapped, frustrated and irritable.

I am able to correct my course by asking myself at any given moment: Is this kind? Are we having fun? What's the brave decision here? How can this become an adventure? Get back into alignment, generate what others have called 'flow' or 'the zone' or a 'positive mental attitude'. It's my peak state — the place from where I achieve the most, enjoy myself the most and create the most joy and pleasure for others.

Your values are unlikely to be exactly the same as mine. Just like the stars in the sky, the things we value are too numerous to count. If I listed them all in this book you'd have a very boring list, so I'm just going to give you a little over 100 words as examples. You might not find all the things you value most in this list, so please don't limit yourself to it. There may be things on this list you are positively repelled by — this is interesting, follow that thought. What's on the other side? What do you think is trampled on, when you look at a 'value' you dislike?

Achievement	Bravery	Daring
Adventure	Calm	Determination
Ambition	Challenge	Devotion
Authenticity	Commitment	Dignity
Awareness	Community	Discipline
Balance	Contribution	Duty
Beauty	Courage	Education
Belonging	Creativity	Empathy
Boldness	Curiosity	Endurance

Entertainment
Excellence
Excitement
Experience
Expressiveness
Fairness
Faith
Fame
Family
Flow
Focus
Freedom
Friendship
Fun
Generosity
Grace
Gratitude
Growth
Happiness
Harmony
Health
Helping
Honesty
Hope
Humour
Imagination
Independence
Integrity
Intimacy
Intuition
Joy
Justice
Kindness

Knowledge
Leadership
Learning
Love
Loyalty
Mastery
Maturity
Mellowness
Moderation
Modesty
Money
Open-minded-
ness
Opportunity
Order
Passion
Peace
Personal-growth
Play
Pleasure
Positivity
Power
Pragmatism
Prosperity
Purpose
Quietness
Reason
Recognition
Relaxation
Respect
Risk
Sacrifice
Safety

Satisfaction
Security
Self-control
Self-respect
Sensuality
Service
Silliness
Spirituality
Stability
Strength
Structure
Sustainability
Teamwork
Thoughtfulness
Thrift
Time
Tolerance
Tradition
Travel
Trust
Unity
Valour
Virtue
Warmth
Wealth
Willingness
Wisdom
Work
Wonder
Worthiness
Zeal

IN YOUR JOURNAL:
THE GIFT OF GETTING THINGS WRONG

When we've spent a long time suppressing or ignoring our own values, picking positive values out of a list of words can be extremely hard. It can sometimes help to connect to happy memories or to examples of role models and people who inspire you by their example. However, I've often found the quickest route to knowing what you *really* care about is by remembering when you were most unhappy.

It's going to take some courage to travel back mentally into those places. Give yourself some time to prepare, and consider the following, before you dive into this next section.

- Are you comfortable?
- Do you have plenty of time to spend on this now?
- Is your journal close at hand?
- Who are you going to call after you've done this exercise?
- Where can you go to lift your spirits as a reward for being courageous?

Cast your mind back to the last time you felt one of the following:
- powerless
- outraged
- humiliated
- bereft
- fearful
- speechless.

Now ask yourself these questions.
- What specifically happened to make you feel this way?
- What important thing was being trampled on, squashed or broken, lost or abandoned in that moment?
- How did this experience challenge you the most?
- What did it cost you?
- Do you feel anger that you allowed this to happen, or panic because you felt unable to prevent it from occurring?
- What did you feel compelled to protect, preserve or reclaim after the event?

The words that come out of your answers will present a very clear picture of what you value most. Our values are the things we feel compelled to protect, those things we are driven to preserve at all costs. They are the principles we are willing to stand for against all the odds and feel most devastated about losing against our will.

I know kindness is my North Star because living with unkindness crushed my spirit. I know that bravery is vital because I cannot live with myself when I fail to take a stand. Adventure matters to me because playing it safe dulled all my aspirations, dreams and hopes for the future. Having fun is something I will go to great lengths to protect for my family because a joyless existence is not one I am prepared to tolerate.

When you have the courage to face your mistakes and embrace the lessons of your life experiences, they will be just that: life experiences. You will no longer wrap up your identity in an experience of abuse, arguments, shame or misery. These can be safely put to one side, with gratitude for what they have taught you.

I learned about integrity by becoming willing to stand up for my own values, no matter who or what was on the line.

I found self-respect by experiencing the freedom of learning how to navigate my own way through my life.

I found joy by releasing the expectation that someone else knew more, or deserved more, than I did myself.

You can learn these things too.

CASE STUDY: CARYS' STORY

Carys came to a group I was running in 2012. She found the values questions extremely challenging indeed. Her whole life she had been encouraged to 'act like a lady', be a 'good girl' and effectively shun her own fiery character in order to attain a kind of feminine ideal. Battling against her own nature had led her into unhappy relationships and unfulfilling roles.

When given the opportunity to voice her own opinions, Carys was completely stuck. "I don't know" was as far as she could get. Carys was furious and embarrassed when she found she literally could not say for herself what mattered in her life. Her every attempt had been framed around someone else's needs.

In the lifelong mission to put other people's needs before her own, Carys had been thoroughly trained to value being praised for her people-pleasing behaviours. Consequently, she

---

sought approval from her partners, her parents and, increasingly, her children. She changed her approach to life often, in line with what she deduced was required of her by each of these key relationships.

Carys was disappearing into martyrdom, not motherhood. Furthermore, she felt isolated in the extreme because not one of the people she loved and cared about the most truly knew or appreciated her for who she really was. Her self-esteem was on a yo-yo string, yanked up and down by whomever she was trying to please in the moment.

There is a deep difference between holding a value of 'service', where you find meaning and contentment and joy from helping others, and being locked into servitude, meeting the needs of others only at a great personal cost to yourself. 'Service' is a value that is often given a 'good' status. People who do 'good work' are lauded and applauded for their selfless attitudes. It's very hard if you have adopted a lifestyle that offers you validation for being 'good' to admit that, deep down, you value something different. Something you might have been taught to label selfish.

For Carys 'recognition' was a powerful value. Substituting recognition in place of service transformed her approach to life. All she needed to do was have the courage to claim it, and give herself permission to admit she believed she had more to offer than simply being a 'good' partner, daughter and mum.

Being recognized by others and enjoying the feeling that you have contributed something valuable to the world through your talents and hard work has just as much meaning as helping others because you love to see them succeed. Neither approach has more value than the other. Each one is valid and rewarding. But each one can become an energy-sapping and miserable existence to the woman who actually values the other.

The fear Carys felt about saying 'This is what I want, need and desire from life' was very real. I know Carys is not alone, and if you feel this way too, do not beat yourself up.

Please Yourself Not Other People

The length and depth of your relationships with people who have undermined you will have a big impact on how fast you are able to identify and put your own values into action. If you had a brief but awful one-off relationship resulting in a child, the impact of this will have been profound, but quite different from the woman who is raised by abusive parents and married for more than 20 years to an abusive man.

Wherever you find yourself on this spectrum, know that there is no competition to be won. Give yourself the kindness of recognizing no-one is standing where you are today. No-one has walked the path you walked to arrive here.

But just as this makes you unique, know that others, whose journeys may look 'worse' or 'easier' than your own, are also unique. Each one of us must find the courage to decide that we are worth it. I cannot measure the amount of courage needed from one mother to the next. All I know is that the well of courage in each of us is deep, and while the decision to draw it up is hard, I have yet to meet a parent who cannot do it.

CASE STUDY: MAGGIE'S STORY

There are certain clients who will always stand out in my memory. I'd like to share with you Maggie's story. Maggie was an older mother when I met her, in her forties with a three-year-old and a baby. She also had two sons from a previous relationship, who were both by then in their early twenties.

Maggie's journey parenting her older sons alone had been a truly difficult path. Swallowed up by a lack of self-worth, with no support systems in place, and lacking the confidence to ask for help, she had found herself with an alcohol addiction midway through their childhood. It's easy to judge Maggie when you're not facing the difficulties she did. But I know, because I have asked, that many, many lone parents look back on their early days of parenting alone and regret the choices they made back then. From shouting too much, to crying too much, to drinking too much, to obsessing about their ex ... there are moments each one of us is not proud of.

Not all parents who wish they had coped better end up with a problem as serious as Maggie had. By the time I met Maggie, she had tackled her addiction, gone some way toward repairing her relationship with her sons, and now had two daughters to take care of — a sober, more experienced mother. Becoming a single parent again was devastating. However, she had no intention of turning to the same coping strategies again.

Maggie took on the challenge of examining her life to discover her values. She attended a live course with me, as part of a group of 12 mothers. In front of all the other women in the group, she courageously told her story.

'My values are pride, independence and self-respect,' Maggie announced. With a tremor in her voice she added, 'I have never said those words to anyone before. I didn't think I had a right to use them after what I did. But this is the real me. I am proud of myself and what I have learned. I won't give up my independence or my self-respect for anyone again. My daughters will know how to respect themselves because they will never see their mother fail to do so.'

Speaking those words mattered a great deal. Beyond simply finding them, in saying them out loud to other people Maggie claimed them for her own. There is an energetic flow to creating change. You may have heard the saying 'If you can see it, you can be it'. Well this is true, but there is slightly more to the process than that!

Maggie saw how far she had come. Building on her own exploration of who she was being and the way she wanted to take leadership of her family, she was able to find those three, powerful words to help her navigate what lay ahead. But it was in speaking those words out loud that Maggie breathed life into them.

As soon as they were out of her mouth and into the room, they had a new kind of energy attached. Witnessed by the people she was sharing the moment with, Maggie's determination to live by these principles became a living thing — it was out of her head and into the world. Now she had spoken them, she was accountable to herself and to the group to make it so.

It was in speaking those words that Maggie also became an artist. The story of her life began to be rewritten. In three words, Maggie started to weave gold through the broken parts of her family history. Ahead of her, those breaks could become celebrated places of learning, honoured aspects of their lives. Places where not only pain had been found, but also purpose.

Speaking Your Truth

When you discover your own set of values make sure that you share them with someone. Take them from your imagination and write them down. Put them on a poster in your living room or your kitchen wall. Talk to your children about what those words mean. Change your computer passwords so you type out these words multiple times a day. If you are parenting teens, ask them to share their own powerful words, discuss what makes your family special and what you each believe your family is united by and stands for.

Your values are not silent ideals to be kept inside your head. They are dynamic, energetic, bright points of light that keep you focused on the pathway ahead. Give them the authority you want them to have and allow them to be known about, talked about, challenged, defended and lived by in your own home. This way you will never lose track of them again.

A Note On Safety

When you think about what you value after having experienced trauma, it is likely that safety will play a leading role. Safety comes first. When you don't feel safe, you can't connect to any of your other values very well. It's hard to feel pride in yourself, or contemplate being brave, or have much fun if you're in fight, flight or freeze mode. If safety is your biggest need right now, that's ok. It's possible to wind down the amygdala (the part of your brain that is responsible for fight or flight reactions) enough to reconnect with the less vigilant parts of yourself.

Clients of mine have been able to identify this yearning for safety in many ways, but one of the loveliest descriptions I've heard is this:

'I want my children to take their home for granted.'

In other words, to have no awareness that their existence is precarious, to feel unthreatened by life when they are at home.

I want this for you as well. Now that you are a lone parent, your home should be your castle. You are the queen and inside these walls you have the right to assert yourself. It is not only ok to ask for what you need, it is essential. Once again, the biggest obstacle here is usually permission — most often, from yourself.

IN YOUR JOURNAL: EXPLORING SAFETY AT HOME

You have the right to feel safe at home. And if you don't feel safe yet, break it down.
- What exactly is making you feel unsafe?
- What needs to happen for you to create a safe space inside your home?
- Who can help you achieve this?
- Where can you take the first step?
- What would you do, if you felt you had the right to do it?

Ensuring your safety at home could mean you need to take legal steps to secure your home from your ex. It could mean establishing rules about your children's behaviour that currently are not in place. It may simply be a shift in your state of mind. Whatever is making you feel unsafe, examine it as thoroughly as you looked at the life experiences we discussed earlier in this chapter. When you give it a name, you can begin to deal with it.

Nebulous feelings of fear will only cut you off from your own true potential. No-one can navigate well in thick fog.

In Your Journal: Values Explored

Think of someone in your life you consider to be a good parent, a role model, someone you trust or respect.

*   What qualities does this person have that you admire?
*   How do you know what matters to them?
*   How does being around them make you feel?

Consider the last time you have felt truly uplifted in your life.

- What was happening when this positive mood arrived?
- What was it that you felt like cherishing or celebrating in that moment?

Look back over your five- or seven-year timeline exercise from the last chapter.
- First look above the line. What do the high points have in common?
- Now look below the line. What do the low points commonly represent?
- How do you decide what is high and what is low in your own life?

Chapter 4

Seeing clearly, living bravely

....

As you think, so shall you be.
Wayne Dyer

....

We have moved around almost a quarter of our coaching cycle by now. This chapter will conclude the rigorous assessment of where you are starting your journey from. The answers you uncover to the questions in this chapter have the power to accelerate your progress exponentially. It is here that we are going to examine your beliefs.

What you believe about the world creates, more than any physical or material thing, the literal edges of your life. Beyond what you believe is possible or acceptable lie the many possible lives that you could not or would not allow yourself to live. If you want something you have never had before, to live a life you have never been able to achieve before, we need to know where your limits currently lie.

And then, we need to move them.

Discovering where your limits are can be a bumpy ride. It's ok, I've been here before — it can get a bit challenging, but I lived to tell the tale. You will too, I promise.

Separating Feelings From Facts

There are some details of my divorce that will forever be burned into my memory. In the emotional meltdown of the end of a relationship, hurtful things are exchanged that have considerable staying power. For me, it was being described as a 'disappointing wife'. This judgement was offered as a justification for my ex-husband's behaviour towards me. I felt the weight of blame, shame and inadequacy heaped upon me at a time I was utterly raw.

To hear yourself described unkindly (or indeed, viciously) by someone you once had loving feelings for is devastating. In this raw emotional state, it's hard to differentiate between fact and fiction. We are not always resilient enough to reject a damning description of ourselves when we hear it at first.

Sometimes, we are so deeply cut that a scar forms around this wound, until it seems a permanent feature of who we now are. 'Disappointing' was a wound like this, for me. I held it close, felt it hurt, wrapped myself around it over time. It became very hard to separate how it felt to be a disappointing person, from how it felt to be me. Disappointing was absorbed by me, ran through me, defined me. I could hardly separate it from my own sense of self.

Over time, experiences and judgements like this get filed in our memories as 'fact' erroneously. The deeper the emotional impact, the more staying power an experience will have. Repetition of an experience will also deepen its effect. Corroboration, in other words when more than one person agrees that something is true, adds further depth and significance to these events. Add up powerful emotional experiences, repeated frequently and corroborated by those we know, like, or trust, (or knew, loved, and trusted once) and you end up with a belief.

Our beliefs are simply opinions and experiences we have had that we now treat as if they are facts.

Both positive and negative life experiences throughout our lives add layer upon layer of information to our own personal version of 'how the world works'. Each one of us believes this manual we've written about life is the gospel truth. After all, it is based on real things we have personally experienced, so it must be right. Right?

Wrong. This is one of those moments when I'm going to ask you to shake up your perspective a little, and it might get a bit uncomfortable. Buckle up and remember — outside your comfort zone is exactly where the magic happens, so if you want the magic, you can handle being uncomfortable.

What Is The Truth?

Truth is a word that carries a lot of weight. To say something is true, we mean that we believe it is accurate, or exact. Rarely are we able to recognize that each one of us will have a slightly different perception of events that have unfolded. My facts are not your facts. However, most people simply experience their lives, interpret that information and treat what they find as a fact.

This insistence that our own personal experiences amount to facts, and an absolute adherence to 'truth', gives rise to conflict. When we believe we are right about something, when we are sure that we know the truth about something, our brains get busy defending this reality.

Why Agree Or Disagree?

Some beliefs are not particularly offensive. Most people will agree on most days that the sky is blue (except when it is grey or white or orange, of course). In fact, the sky being blue is more like an agreement. We agree that the sky is mostly blue, most of the time, so if someone asks you what colour it is …

you're likely to say blue. Even if right now the sky you are standing underneath … isn't.

This kind of agreement about what is real can also be described as a social contract. It makes life slightly easier if we can socially and culturally agree about certain things. Agreeing that the default colour of the sky is blue means we can all go about our business day by day focusing on other things, sidestepping pointless discussions or arguments about whether this is true (or accurate, or exact).

Thus, we see that a shared belief works in a predictable way: we all form opinions, then most people treat the consensus like a fact. But why? Why do we state opinions that are demonstrably not always 'true', as if they were facts? Well, first of all, treating this opinion like a fact saves time and energy and allows us to focus on other, more important things instead.

In this way, it is easy to see how social, personal and cultural beliefs are fundamentally important to our ability to function in our daily lives. We all need to be able to focus on more important things in any given moment. As tiny children we had to form opinions about what was safe and learn about how to behave in order to survive. The information we downloaded from our caregivers and environments added up to a rule book. A manual for life specific to the spaces, places and relationships that we needed to conform to the most.

The Rules

Inside each of our rule books there are three distinct categories:

- beliefs about ourselves
- beliefs about other people
- beliefs about how the world works.

These beliefs are rarely questioned. As well as keeping us safe and helping us belong to our social group, beliefs act as a filter for the mass of information hurtling at us every day. Knowing the sky is blue means that you do not have to pay attention to the sky. You know exactly what colour it should be and that is good enough to get by, so you can afford to skip over the details.

Blue skies are hardly worth worrying about. But some of our other beliefs deserve to be paid close attention. This chapter is all about examining your own rule book for life and uncovering what opinions you are treating like facts. It's vital that you do this and do it honestly, because the beliefs we unconsciously hold mean we skip over the process of making a deeply considered response to life. Our beliefs are custom built to make us take short cuts.

Just for a moment imagine the short cuts I took back when I accepted as fact the claim that I was a 'disappointing' wife. What I might have come to accept about the limits of my own potential, my own worth and, by extension, my right to enjoy a happy and fulfilling family life. I am grateful that I was able ultimately to reject this opinion and release the belief. Now imagine for a moment I had not and how holding on to the belief that I was a fundamentally disappointing person might have impacted on my children over time.

Trauma and pain will have wounded you. If you have scars that you need to soften, you are not alone. Go back to your values again: be kind, claim your self-respect, connect with your own celestial point in this moment.

The person you are becoming made it through this difficult journey. The mother who raised happy, confident children who love life found a way to face her fears. You are an artist and a storyteller today. Remember that one day soon, your scars will be seams of gold, and the woman who wears them will be a powerful visionary in charge of her life.

What's Your Default Setting?

Some people have truly empowering beliefs. They believe that they are clever, strong, beautiful and loved. They believe other people are fundamentally good, generous, kind and welcoming. They believe the world is full of opportunity, possibility and beauty.

Some, on the other hand, have limiting and obstructive beliefs. They believe they are stupid, ugly and unworthy. That other people are cruel, superior, judgemental and mean. That the world is a dangerous, miserable place that offers no pleasure or contentment or safety.

Which one of these people is working on an objective 'truth'? Can either claim that their perspective on life is universally accurate, or exact? In my experience neither perspective is really true. But I know which one I would rather have.

And I know what it feels like to have the one that makes you miserable.

Our beliefs do not just land in our laps as gifts from the universe. They come from predictable sources that can be tracked back through time. If you want to understand why you don't feel good enough, strong enough or worthy enough to claim your absolute right to authority and the artistry of your family, this chapter is for you

Gifts From People We Know And Places We Go

Your beliefs will have come from one of three places:

- from people you know, love or like and trust
- from your upbringing, your society and culture, including the media, your education and your immediate environment
- from your own direct life experiences — the things you have lived through, personally witnessed, felt or done.

Let's take a look at these, one by one.

The category of beliefs that stem from people you know, love, like or trust is very emotionally charged. These beliefs can carry you through life on a golden cloud of positivity or, conversely, mire you in a pit of self-doubt and despair.

IN YOUR JOURNAL:
BELIEFS GIFTED BY PEOPLE

Think about your own parents, your friends or your teachers when you were young. What did they tell you about yourself?
- Did they tell you that you were smart, lovable and fun?

- Did they enjoy your company and value spending time with you?
- When you achieved something important did they celebrate with you?
- When you felt something painful, did they show you how much they cared?

This is the birthplace of self-worth. A shaky start can be overcome in later life, but it certainly matters if your early years were filled with a sense of love and security. Knowing you were loved translated into a belief that you are lovable. This alone is a gift of immeasurable worth. What value can any of us place on deeply believing, in our gut, that it is true, accurate, exact, that I am worthy of love?

If your childhood did not give you this gift, you will have felt its absence even if you did not know it was something you lacked. Never knowing if you are worthy of love, or deserving of happiness, safety and celebration leaves us open to relationships that overtly or covertly abuse us.

Of course, not all children who have a rough childhood will go on to be adults who are abused. And not all who are carried in that golden cloud of positivity will be immune to a darker future. But it is important to recognize that our beliefs are formed this early on. It is the unconscious trust we have in the people around us to tell us the truth about the world that leads us to accept as facts things which may or may not, in fact, be true.

In later life, our intimate relationships replicate this pattern. As we fall in love and form new bonds with partners, our young adult brains go through a period of testing out what is true. As we learn how to be intimate within adult relationships, our brains again become uniquely open to the opinions of others. The way we are received in these relationships has the power to re-wire the way we think about ourselves.

In Your Journal: Beliefs Gifted By People Continued

Now think about the people you have been closest to in your early adult life. The lovers, the partners, the most trusted friends.

- Did they tell you they loved you, often?
- Did they show you with their actions that you were worthy of their time?
- Did they cherish the gifts of your body or energy or effort?
- Did they celebrate all you could be in the world?

A lover or partner or friend can heal the hurts of a bad childhood. Just as easily a bad set of friends or a bad relationship can destroy your self-belief and self-worth. If you had the misfortune of both a shaky start and traumatic adult relationships then know this now: the opinions you hold about the world today are not 'true'. They are neither accurate, nor exact. Nor are they fixed for all time.

'Here And There', 'Us And Them', 'Mine And Yours'

Your upbringing was infused with a second layer of opinions that seeped into your unconscious mind. The social and cultural conditioning each of us experience as children paints a picture of what is 'normal'. These experiences tell us where to find meaning in our lives, what is acceptable, what is beautiful, what is allowed.

Just take a moment to think about what 'normal' life looks like to you. Now, think about the incredible kaleidoscope of opinions and attitudes our diverse world contains. In one culture, the colour white signifies virginity and purity; in another, white is reserved for death. In one society, curves are the physical ideal; in another, the waif reigns supreme. In this culture, families live together in multi-generational homes; in that one, young couples live alone hundreds of miles from their parents, aunts and uncles. Here, cohabiting is acceptable; there, cohabiting will see you shunned as a sinner.

These ideas of belonging and otherness are constructed in our childhood too. The way your family lived, the norms of your culture, faith or community … these experiences gave you edges to your world. They told you where you fit in and what was expected of you. They also told you who was welcome and who was not, and what behaviour would lead to adulation, or to shame.

These structures and constructs shaped everything about who you became today, whether you embraced them or rejected them wholesale.

If your life today falls outside of the boundaries you were taught were 'normal', complicated feelings will arise. It may be a vague and unsettling sense of feeling conflicted about yourself. You may be unsure if you are allowed to like your own life, or enjoy how it has turned out. Or it may be explicit. Your community may literally have closed its doors to you, shunned you and exiled you from all that you once held dear.

To you I also offer hope. Normal is as kaleidoscopic as the communities around our globe. You can be sure you are not the only person like you, living the way your life has turned out. The loss of identity, belonging and community is a tangible grief that you are entitled to spend time mourning.

Know that, on the other side of grief, there is a new life waiting for you. It will never be the same as the life you had before, and you may never be able to forget that you have suffered this disconnection. But you can and will discover a way to live outside of the parameters you once had. The first step is allowing yourself to grieve, the next is giving yourself permission to stop.

When Your Beliefs Are Founded On Proof

Of all the ways we form beliefs, our direct life experiences carry a literal punch. In the space of a few seconds something can happen that snatches away everything you once believed was true and rewrites your rule book in an instant.

Clients have shared many versions of these moments with me. Perhaps you will have experienced one of these life-altering events yourself:

- discovering your husband was abusing your child
- finding out that your partner had another family in another town
- being punched or kicked by the man who had told you he loved you

- being denied access to your own money, destitute at the hands of your husband or partner
- being prevented from taking care of your baby when she cried.

There are many terrible and traumatic things that give us a 'sliding-door' moment, the sensation that you have slipped from one world where you knew what was true, reliable and safe, into a parallel universe where nothing is as you once believed it was. Not yourself, not other people, not the world.

These are shattering experiences to have. However resilient your foundations may have been, however golden the cloud of your childhood, these are not moments anyone simply bounces back from.

If you are reeling from the shock and horror of something this terrible, know that you are allowed to be utterly floored by this experience. No-one expects you to have an answer to what has happened to you. It's normal to need time to recover.

You will recover.

I know you will because alongside those experiences that blow our worlds apart, there are others that put them back together again. The surest way to heal from the literal and metaphorical punches of life is to patiently, skillfully, artfully learn to look for gold. For every terrible experience you have had, seek out five that counteract it.

If you felt abandoned and unworthy of love, building relationships will bring you peace.

If you felt diminished, powerless and discarded, being of service to the world and contributing your gifts to others will remind you that you are a person who has value today.

If you felt frightened, broken, paralyzed by fear, claiming your right to take action for your own good will heal your pain.

Not fast, not in the flick of a switch. I can't promise to turn your lights on as fast as they were once turned out, but I can share stories that might show you were to begin.

CASE STUDY: ISOBEL'S STORY

Isobel cried her way through the first three days of her retreat. Not big, attention-grabbing tears. Silent, please-don't-notice-me tears. With shaking hands, she steadfastly wrote down what we discussed and refused to make eye contact.

Isobel's relationships had given her layer upon layer of beliefs about herself, other people and the world. The drip, drip, drip of negative comments from her partner and the father of her three children had soaked through all her positivity, leaving her convinced that she was unattractive, stupid, weak, pathetic, worthless.

Although hindsight showed with clarity how cruel he had been, during their relationship Isobel had not been able to see his flaws, only her own. The cut-off point was discovering a secret that blew their world apart. In that moment, everything imploded.

She made the decision to end the relationship. As a military wife, she was then required to vacate their married quarters, move off base and begin again. Without financial resources of her own and with three children to protect and the shock of the discovery to deal with, this period of time was her own personal version of hell.

Out in an unfamiliar world without the companionship of the regiment's other wives and the structure of military life, Isobel was bewildered. She had little to call her own. Her identity had been snatched away — who was she without all the things that life had contained? Not having an external way to validate herself, and having such a low internal sense of value, Isobel naturally expected rejection from her peers and community. In her mind, there was nothing about her left that made her interesting or valuable at all.

> I could see all the years of emotional abuse she had suffered at the hands of her ex. These mental wounds had been internalized as facts. It wasn't yet clear to Isobel that she could choose to reject his opinions about who she was.
>
> Someone else's opinion is only that, an opinion. Someone else's actions are not your responsibility. We do not need to accept what is put in front of us.

Raising The Bar

You may have learned, like Isobel, to lower your expectations of yourself, your partner, or even of the world itself. Know that as your expectations lower, the bar you set for yourself sinks with it. This matters because we rarely question the things we expect to find.

Once upon a time Isobel expected to be cherished. Once upon a time, she expected to feel safe. Once upon a time, she expected to be loved. Bit by bit, she had lowered those expectations. As the bar dropped, she had found herself accepting less and less and less.

Our job when we worked together was to raise that bar again, so that never again would she accept the scraps of a relationship with a man, or with herself again. We started in the places Isobel had the most power. We started with tiny, incremental changes. Changes that required almost no energy. Small actions that on their own appeared to amount to nothing at all.

Perhaps you don't believe that nail polish can heal a broken heart. I won't blame you if you don't. But this is where we began. Isobel committed to doing something that showed herself love every day. She agreed that she would stop simply accepting that she would feel worthless every morning. She agreed to raise that bar, maybe only inches at a time, but up, up and up. To stop expecting rejection and instead, stand tall and meet someone else's eyes today. To dress like she cared about herself. To put nail polish on again, because she liked to.

Something appalling had shattered her family life into a mosaic of little pieces. In the scattered mess she found herself adrift in, Isobel discovered it was the tiny things that would help stitch the pieces back together. Taking the time to smile, to cook, to cuddle her children, to connect with life again.

With every loving action Isobel took for her own wellbeing, she sent an intention out into the world. She claimed a tiny part of her heart back, and took up a little more space for her own happiness. As her confidence grew, her children began to relax and thrive with her again. They laughed again.

You are more than the sum of what has happened to you. You are allowed to have high expectations, even if you have been let down. The person who let you down is at fault. Your expectations of safety, love and fairness were not to blame. In fact, it is by restoring your high expectations that you will be safe again.

Think of it like limbo dancing. When you keep on lowering the bar, all you are doing is getting closer to falling down in the mud. Raise that bar? You'll one day be able to walk tall, shoulders back and sail right on through.

CASE STUDY: KANDY'S STORY

Kandy was midway through legal proceedings with her ex when we met. A combination of divorce and child-arrangement issues needed to be resolved. Progress was painfully slow, and Kandy was sure that her ex was deliberately obstructing each process to make sure that she spent as much money as possible and that it all took an inordinate amount of time.

Kandy was angry, understandably so. But one day she said something that unlocked a whole new world of possibility.

'I just want to be divorced so I can move on with my life!'

'Ok', I said, 'I understand. Tell me about that. What will change when you are divorced? What needs to happen for this to be done?'

We talked it through piece by piece.

Financially, nothing would alter that wasn't already in process. The children were unlikely to have a dramatic change in their living situation or contact arrangements. There would be no knock-on effect to where or how Kandy actually lived.

The block, she discovered, was almost entirely emotional. Yet Kandy still had a deeply held belief that getting her decree absolute would cut the ties she had with her husband and release her from that life.

As we methodically worked through the physical and material ties Kandy retained with her ex, she realized each one could in fact be severed sooner than the document could be procured.

The belief that this piece of paper would allow her to feel divorced was simply an opinion she had formed that was now masquerading as a fact. In reality, unless Kandy began the process of emotionally releasing herself from the relationship now, in the moment she was in today, then that paper would have no more power to render her divorced than a piece of tissue would.

She could choose to be divorced today. Once the emotional block was released, all that remained was the administrative tasks. 'Moving on with her life' was not something for which she needed her ex's permission, or a legal document. She only really needed her own permission. With a simple shift in her perspective, her whole reality changed. The same amount of administrative tasks remained. The financial cost and physical process could not be significantly changed. However, the emotional burden could be set down there and then.

So it was.

IN YOUR JOURNAL: FEELINGS ARE NOT FACTS

Set aside some time and sit with your journal. Release any expectations you have about what may come out when you do this exercise. It is likely that when you start writing you will uncover a mix of both positive and negative beliefs.

This exercise works best when you write relatively quickly and with no self-censoring.

Remember no-one will see your answers. They are only being recorded so you can become aware of them.

Take each one of these sentences and start a new page. Complete them as many times as you can, each time with a new answer.

- Parenting by myself is …
- My children are …
- My ex-partner is …
- My support network is …
- The world is …
- I am …

Take a break when you are done. This whole exercise should take about 30 minutes. Come back to the pages you have written after a little time away and read back what you have written.

- Are the things you have written opinions?
- If they are, whose opinions are they? Did they come from someone else before you adopted them as your own?
- If these opinions actually belong to someone else, do you like, trust, respect and believe that person today? Would you ask them for advice today or accept their perspective as truth?
- Are you sure that what you have recorded is fact?

- Where is the evidence for these statements being fact?
- How do you know they are true (accurate, exact)?
- Are they actually only true some of the time, just like blue (grey, white or orange) skies?

You will likely discover that your answers represent a spectrum of opinions that have been formed by you, based on what people you knew, loved, liked and trusted (even if you no longer love, like or trust them) have told you. Influenced by your own cultural and social conditioning. Altered by your direct life experiences.

Viewed through this lens, you can claim these opinions or — crucially — you can choose to reject them. You have the right to self-edit, review and remove beliefs that no longer serve you.

If this list does not represent your best life, here's what you need to do.

1 Seek out new people whom you love, like and trust today and allow them to encourage you, support you and nurture you on your journey. As far as is possible remove people who do not give you what you need in your life.

2   Take a critical eye to the things you consume socially and culturally. Does what you watch, read and listen to make you feel good or bad about yourself? What can you bring into your environment that enhances your life instead? What can you release?

3   Seek out new life experiences that affirm you. Start small. Evolution is more sustainable than revolution. The power of shocking or stressful life experiences can be limited simply by stacking up positive experiences that counteract how the bad ones have made you feel. What can you do right now, today, to make you feel good? Proud? Loved? Find your power. Even if it is as small as putting polish on your nails!

Remember this when you reflect on the beliefs you have uncovered in this chapter: childhood, cultural and family beliefs are almost never given to us with the intention of causing us pain. Releasing the legacy of your family or cultural suffering can be incredibly powerful, and does not require you to reject or condemn those you love.

As an adult, we are able to examine our experiences with a critical eye in a way that we were unable to do as children. If you find that you no longer agree with how your parents lived or raised you, if you look back on the way your loved ones taught you to view the world and feel angry or sad, try to remember they were doing the best that they could with what they had. Your parents, carers and community were all operating from the rule books they had been gifted by their own experiences. None of us is perfect, none of us owns the truth.

All we can do is accept each other compassionately while having the courage to challenge ourselves.

Part Two

What Do I Want Next?

And will you succeed?
Yes! You will, indeed!
(98 and ¾ percent guaranteed)
Dr Seuss

Congratulations! Stop for a moment and take a breath. You have done some amazing work so far. You now know who you have been being up till now, what you value most and what's been holding you back.

Have you ever taken such a thorough inventory of your own life? If not take it from me, it's a huge deal. I'm proud of you. You deserve to be proud of yourself. If you've not congratulated yourself yet, do something now to say well done — a metaphorical high five for yourself! Acknowledge the investment you've made in 'you' already.

After you've had a glass of bubbly or, if you're like me, a cup of tea and biscuit (a very British celebration), it will be time to roll up your sleeves again.

We're entering part two of your journey, spinning around the coaching cycle into more action-oriented steps. This is where you're going to explore your options. Draw up a rough guide to where you're heading and stick a pin in 'What do I want next?'

Chapter 5

Inspiration or desperation?

Leadership requires two things: a vision of the world that does not yet exist and the ability to communicate it.
Simon Sinek, *Start with Why: How Great Leaders Inspire Everyone to Take Action*

In the next few chapters you will learn how to develop a vision of your life that does not exist yet, how to communicate that vision to other people and how to identify the people and resources that will help you as you set off on this next phase of your life.

But before we go charging into action, there's one more thing to establish first. Why are you going to create a vision for your family and actively work to manifest this new reality?

In my experience, there are two things that motivate people into taking serious action to change their lives. The first is inspiration, and the second is desperation. It would be wonderful if we were all motivated by inspiration alone to do amazing things, but the truth is that, more often than not, we change our lives because not changing them has become incredibly uncomfortable. We have reached a place where the pain of staying where we are outweighs the pain of trying something new.

If this is true for you, you're in good company. When I sat down in January 2013 at 8 p.m. with a cup of tea in hand, a good friend by my side, my nine-month-old baby and two-year-old toddler asleep in bed … I wrote my first business plan in a blend of both of these states.

I was inspired by the idea of financial independence and the freedom to work around my kids. I was also terrified of living solely on benefits, in a house I didn't believe I could afford, with no way to pay for any childcare for my boys. I was afraid of living my own version of groundhog day, staring down the barrel at an endless string of days rolling out ahead of me where little could meaningfully change. Indeed, I was fearful of settling into a life where I lacked the finances, resources or skills to move us forward by myself.

Knowing I could be completely financially dependent upon the state and a 24/7 single mum was truly scary for me. I am not a stay-at-home-mother by nature. While I adore my children with a fierce love, I need to be by myself, working on something else, at least some of the time, to be happy.

Recognizing what it takes for you to be truly happy is the key to taking action that transforms your life for the better. Taking any action at all will certainly create motion. But only certain actions will help you to find happiness. Your own personal version of a happy life may be the exact opposite of mine, or so far from any ideas I would be inspired to have, that I couldn't begin to suggest your next steps.

As your coach, it's really important that I emphasize now that your best life is utterly unique. Replicating someone else's version of 'the good life' is pointless. This is not the time to ask people around you for advice or suggestions as to what to do next. Now is the time to dig deep and work out exactly what, for you, happiness could look like.

IN YOUR JOURNAL:
BE, DO, HAVE

Sit down now and make a list of everything you want to Be, Do and Have in your life in ten years' time. You'll need a minimum of 15 minutes, a clear head, a pen and your journal. If you're with your children right now, wait until you have time by yourself to do this. It's important to be able to focus on this activity.

Complete these sentences as many times as you possibly can, each time with a new answer. Only when you've exhausted all your ideas should you move on.

- I will be …
- I will do …
- I will have …

When you're done, start again.

This time, include your children in your answers.

- We will be …
- We will do …
- We will have …

Set no limits. Have fun with this! If you find you are inspired to imagine winning the lottery or to employ staff to wait on you at home hand and foot — record it! If you want to run a six-figure business (or grow the one you already have), work for a specific company, retrain for your dream job … don't hold back. If joy to you means a two-up two-down cottage in the country with just your cat and your children, baking bread or walking the dogs, own it and write it on your list! Keep going.

No-one is judging you but you. Life can be re-imagined. Nothing is stopping your brain from being creative, other than the limits you are setting yourself.

Ask yourself these questions.

- What would you really want life to look like if you were honest with yourself?
- What secret desires do you have, that have perhaps been hidden for a very long time?
- If money, time and experience were no obstacle, what would you honestly dream of being, doing and having in your life?
- What makes your heart sing, your eyes smile and your soul laugh?

Ok! All done. Time to take a breather. Step away from all the things that you have written for at least half an hour if you can. Better still, for a day.

You may have several ideas buzzing around your mind right now, if you've allowed yourself truly to get into a state of possibility. Perhaps you are feeling energized and excited.

However, it may be that you're not able to get there today. Perhaps inspiration has not arrived yet. That's ok too. If your list is all about desperation, that is a valid starting point too. Take all your negative statements (anything that sums up what you don't want) and find a way to reword them positively. You may need to practise giving yourself permission in order really to let loose!

CASE STUDY: MILLIE'S STORY

Millie didn't want to be bored. She absolutely didn't want to remain stuck in the 'good job' her family thought would give her security. She didn't want to be a single mother to only one child forever. But she also didn't want to be tied down in a relationship either. It took several attempts at flipping the 'no thank you' statements to find the 'yes please!' statements that could take their place.

Eventually Millie found answers that even surprised herself. Yes please to a nomadic lifestyle. Yes please to travelling with her young son. Yes please to home educating around this carefree existence. Yes please to rejecting a traditional life. Yes please to believing she was entitled to have dreams that suited her personality, not dreams cut down to size by her current situation. Yes please to believing that she and her son deserved to be happy, free and having fun.

I know that your dreams are alive and well inside you right now. But they may be doing a good job of hiding out under the weight of other people's expectations, and the pressures that come with the transition into parenting alone.

If this is the case for you, the Be, Do, Have exercise may feel like heavy lifting. Give yourself a chance and try to do it anyway — you won't know how strong, creative and passionate you can be until you try.

Being Realistic Is The Quickest Way To Kill Your Dreams

Whatever has come up for you in this exercise, notice it as much as possible without judging it as good or bad. Consider your starting point today (whether you feel resourced or struggling, whether you feel safe and secure or under threat, whether you have a network around you or not). Think about the historic influences of your closest relationships (partners and your own parents especially). Consider the current state of your separated family. Are you still in legal conflicts? Is contact safe, regular and established? All these things will have a big impact on what you feel is possible for you now.

Many of my clients have initially struggled to let go and embrace the more creative ideas this exercise asks of you the first time round. 'Realism' is often the sticking point.

CASE STUDY: JOANNA'S STORY

Joanna's story is a great example of rising above realism, even at a time when it seems impossible or pointless to do so. Joanna was negotiating the division of assets in a very acrimonious divorce when we met. The parameters seemed to be very much set in stone. There was a specific amount of money to be divided. Four children to keep in their respective schools left little wiggle room for relocation. Joanna's own business required a great deal of her mental energy above and beyond the work of separation. Reinvention (as far as she was concerned) was definitely off the table.

On the surface of it, Joanna was a tremendously impressive woman. She not only worked for herself, but employed other people, ran her own household and was doing a great job of raising four children between the ages of five and seventeen. Her life, to anyone giving it a superficial glance, could even be considered aspirational, despite her divorce.

But Joanna had spent years suffering in silence in a miserable marriage. Constantly put down by her husband, financially taken advantage of and undermined in front of their children, Joanna's self-esteem when we began working together was at rock bottom. While others congratulated her on keeping everything going, she was quietly crying inside. From the outside looking in, her life looked rosy. But from the inside looking out, Joanna only saw grey.

'Realistic' for Joanna was continuing to work flat out in her business, keeping her public face smiling and her private mask in place to protect the children. She had come to believe that moving house was a bad, if not impossible, idea. In order to keep all her dependants (in business and at home) secure, Joanna was willing to shelve her own dreams completely. If ever there was a swan who was frantically paddling under the water, Joanna was one.

In the ten weeks it took us to work through the programme, Joanna managed to shift her perspective on 'realistic' from maintaining the status quo to creating a staggeringly different life.

After considerable encouragement, she agreed to write the Be, Do, Have list out as a complete fantasy. No timeline attached or even factored in. Purely for fun. Her defining question became 'What would I do if nothing was holding me back?'

Once she released the emotional block of realism and wrote truthful answers down, Joanna saw in black and white opportunities that she'd simply not allowed herself to see before.

On her list Joanna had written 'I will have roses around my door'. When we discussed it together, Joanna qualified this desire by adding 'in 20 years from now'. In reality, it took less than 20 weeks to find a house that fulfilled her dream, because once the dream became a goal, she allowed herself to look for it in real life.

Once her financial settlement concluded, she moved into her dream cottage with her children, just a short commute from the children's schools. She paid off her mortgage in full, dropped her working hours by ten, promoted an employee who was thrilled to up their game. 'Realistic' transformed in front of her very eyes when she let go of the idea that how your life looks today is how it must continue to look.

IN YOUR JOURNAL:
CHALLENGE ALL THE AGREEMENTS YOU MADE WITH REALITY

If being realistic is holding you back, take a look at the last chapter again. Reality is simply a concept with which you have decided to agree. Realistic means something different for me than it does for you. Take a good long look at where your version of 'realistic' has come from.

- Who told you what you could expect to be, do, have or achieve up till now?
- What evidence are you focusing on to back up this 'realistic' perspective?
- What evidence can you find from your own life that doesn't support this view?
- What unrealistic things have you achieved in your own lifetime already?
- What did it take for you to believe those things were, in fact, possible?
- How would it feel to reject a realistic, limited view of your own potential?

These are tough questions to ask yourself. All kinds of emotions are likely to arise. If they do and you need a break, set down realism for the day, then come back and write your Be, Do, Have list again tomorrow if you need to.

When you rewrite your list, focus on the potential you feel you have on your best day, not your worst day. Approach it from a perspective of possibilities, not limits.

Moving From What To Why

Most people only get as far as describing what they want. And as you've already discovered, that alone can be quite a feat! But even if you do know what you want, on its own your what will not transform a series of goals into a compelling vision. If you share only what you want with your children, it is unlikely to inspire them to do more, be more or achieve more with their own lives. A list of material goals will rarely move any group of people toward unified action for change — least of all a traumatized family still reeling from a huge change in their circumstances. So let's take a step back and look through a different lens.

When business coach Simon Sinek asked business leaders to 'start with why', he was challenging business men and women to build their organization around a 'big why'. Why does their organization exist, and why do they do what they do? Do their reasons inspire and excite them? I'd like to apply the 'big why' to your family right now.

What if you could view your family without the emotional maelstrom of guilt, stress, passion or emotion that families often inspire? What if you could look at your family, just for a moment, as an organization that is waiting for a 'big why' to bring you closer together? Now, imagine what it would be like for your family to share a purpose-driven life. To be in agreement about the things you all value most. Pulling together to head in the direction of a happy, shared life.

Sinek asked business people to think about leadership with these words: 'If your actions inspire others to dream more, learn more, do more and become more, you are a leader.'

Let's just sit with that idea for a moment and think about parenting as a leadership role. Do you want your children to dream more, learn more, do more and become more? Do you want to be the person who guides them toward fulfilling and most importantly happy lives? Would you like to be happy yourself while you do all of that?

I've yet to meet a parent who has said no.

In truth, most of the parents I work with are very motivated to give their children a better life. It may have been one of the major reasons, if not the reason, they became a single parent in the first place. But does better automatically mean happier? Better may mean safer or materially more secure, or all manner of good and worthy things. However, it isn't always synonymous with happier. A happier life might mean even letting go of some of the measures that you use right now to determine if life as a lone parent family is 'better'.

Learning To Lead With Love

Parenting is, I believe, the most intense and necessary form of leadership there is. It is a form of leadership you are engaged in right now, whether or not you want to be or realize you are. Which is why the journey you are making is a blend of seeking beauty mixed with claiming your authority. I am asking you to think hard about what leading your family means to you.

For the mother I had become after a year or more of conflict, drama and despair, it was invigorating to be set this challenge. What would it take for me to become the visionary, the trailblazer, the safe pair of hands on my family's future? To throw off the habit not only of thinking about myself in a limiting and negative way, but actively to live a life without negativity and limits.

Before you set any personal or family goals in stone, realize that claiming your leadership and authority as a parent is no longer optional. You must step into this leadership identity and make it your own. Try it on for size and begin to stretch the definition of leadership you may have started with, until it becomes something that fits you like a glove.

If Not You, Then Who?

If you are uncomfortable or uneasy in any way with stepping into your role as leader of your family, I have one question for you.

Who are you deferring to?

Is it your ex-partner? Your own parents? Your friends, wider family or community? Your child's peer group, teachers, club leaders or friends? Which of these people are you willing to pass your responsibility to, to allow to set the tone for how life in your family will be lived?

Because, make no mistake, without your strong and loving leadership at home, one of these people will become the person your child turns to for guidance in your stead. When they are searching for their own bright stars to navigate by, how brightly you shine as a guide will make all the difference. The lights held out to them by other people will always be attractive, and can be amazing complements to your own.

But if you in any way abdicate your responsibility to shine a light of your own, your child will have a much harder time working out which of the many others he is going to follow.

The Spark Of 'Why?'

We're going to begin to flex those leadership muscles now, by reviewing your Be, Do and Have list.

As I've explained above, each of us can explain what we want for our families once we give ourselves the opportunity to do so without self-censorship. However, the parents who create powerful, life-changing visions for their family's future are the ones who can also articulate why.

Set aside any anxieties about how for now — the next chapter is completely dedicated to helping you work out that step.

IN YOUR JOURNAL:
TAKE YOUR TIME REVIEWING YOUR
BE, DO, HAVE LIST

For each and every thing you have written down, as outlandish or understated as it may be, ask yourself *why*.

- Why do I want this in my/our future?
- What do I believe this thing will give me or my children?

- Why is this important to me?
- Is this, in fact, still important to me, now I look at it again?
- What would achieving this thing (however fantastical) in real life represent to me?
- How would this improve our lives?
- Why is that an outcome I care about?

Your why answers will end up being a list of single words.

Words like happiness, freedom, security, safety, independence or belonging. Words that look just like your list of personal values.

An Aligned Life In Action

Once you can see your 'why's in black and white on paper, something magical happens. Compare them to your values and join up the dots.

Here in front of you is the germ of the 'how' we will uncover in the next chapter. See how it is possible that a series of aligned choices can add up to the dream life you dared to describe. Understand how making those choices consistently can in fact accelerate your journey exponentially toward an amazing new version of reality.

If you can take even the first small steps toward your why, your values, the things you hold most dear, this will gift you with a greater degree of happiness. Living a life where these principles are reflected in each of your actions will soon feel like a dream come true.

You may find that you don't need a specific car, or job, or house or income level to feel the sense of freedom, pride, achievement or fun that these items may have represented for you on your what list. You can take any action in the direction of fun, freedom, pride or achievement and begin to experience the happiness of being in your aligned state, in the here and now.

The Gratitude Gift

The happiest people are able to find something to be grateful for exactly where they find themselves at any given time.

I know that I'm asking you to undertake a big shift in perspective here, given the situations that led you to pick up this book. It's hard to be grateful for a callous, cruel or absent ex, an abusive relationship or a separation marked by conflict, violence or uncertainty. There is precious little to find to celebrate when the focus remains on any of these things.

The gravitational pull of this black hole of misery can and must be severed. You are completely capable of being the woman who falls back in love with her life — today you're going to do two things with me to make this so.

IN YOUR JOURNAL: GATHERING YOUR JAR OF STARS

- Identify five things you are grateful for right now, today, in your life. Exactly as your life is in this moment.
- Write these down on strips of paper.
- Find a Kilner jar or similar container in which to keep these gratitude gifts.
- You can roll them up, fold them up or, if origami is your thing, hop on over to my website www.ninafarr.com and look up the blog post titled 'jar of stars'. Here you will find out how to fold them into cute little lucky bubble stars.

Commit to recording the things you are grateful for, proud of, wish to celebrate as a family, every day from here on forward. Involve your children too. At the end of every day, if each one of you puts something into your jar of stars, you will very quickly begin to see how your life is full of things that make you happy, right here, right now, just as you are.

- As time goes on, practise paying attention to the things both you and your children want to record in this way.
- Do they match the why you identified?
- What makes you all feel happy and connected as a family, right here, right now?
- Practise looking for opportunities to recreate and develop these happy moments at home.
- Reflect on this question. What can you do right now, today, starting exactly where you are, to begin moving in the direction of your happiest, aligned life?

Building Bricks By Hand

Many of us yearn for progress that is out of step with the pace at which we can honestly achieve change. You may well wish for a completely different life to materialize out of thin air right now and I admit that my heart ached for that not so long ago too. But today we are not asking a fairy godmother to conjure us up castles in the clouds.

Today we are simply building our own bricks by hand.

Every small step you take in alignment with your values, each move however tiny that brings you closer to your why, is a brick which will eventually be used by you to build you own castle.

Consider making just five small bricks a day, every day for a week ... a month ... a year ... five years.

I am writing this book five years and three months from the day I wrote my very first vision for my newly fractured family. I am nearly 10,000 bricks closer to building my own personal castle, and I have got this far because I know my why. I can promise you that writing a book was not in my original vision for myself, nor found on my what list. Because the what has unfolded thanks to the why ... not the other way around.

Just imagine what you could do with 10,000 bricks of your own. Each tiny action — recording your gratitude, tuning into your happiness, acknowledging your hopes and aspirations — will turn you into the hero of your own story — and, more importantly, into the visionary leader your family needs you to be today.

Chapter 6

Alone is not lonely

Love is not patronizing and charity isn't about pity, it is about love. Charity and love are the same ...
Mother Theresa

'No man is an island' declared John Donne some 400 years ago. I believe he was on to something. No man or woman can function on their own away from the loving embrace of their wider community. You are no exception to this rule. With the greatest of love, I'm here to encourage you to adjust your view again to include the world outside your door — and to get excited about meeting it full on.

In this phase of the coaching cycle, you will be invited to begin trying out new approaches to life. Standing on the sidelines or overthinking things will only hold you back, so be willing to suck at this. Trying something new isn't about nailing it first time. Being willing to try a new approach to a sticky problem is about finding out what your options are. In exploring your options, you will also learn where your strengths lie and become willing to develop your skills if your current resources aren't serving you or your family so well.

Let's begin by taking stock. This journey has been jam-packed with progress already. You have figured out what your personal values are, and reinforced this discovery by layering up your values with some goals that represent happiness to you. You've demolished the rule book that you once allowed to limit your one, wonderful and extraordinary life. You've done the work to dare to dream. Now we're rolling up our sleeves and getting stuck in.

Forward motion requires that you step purposefully in the direction of your dreams.

It's ok! I know this is where a lot of my clients panic.

But a purposeful step is only a step. A single brick. One deliberately crafted decision at a time. I'm not asking you to be a wonder woman, only to become your own best advocate.

Advocacy And Delegation

An advocate is someone who calls in aid, argues on behalf of a cause, summons or invites others to help. Becoming an advocate for yourself and your family is the rocket boost your lone parent loveliness needs right now. As an advocate, you will find lone parenting is no longer lonely. You can lay down once and for all the idea of 'pulling double duty' 'being Mum and Dad' or 'fighting the good fight'. We're done with all of that. As an advocate, you're going to be the kind of leader who builds a team.

The team you need around your family is almost certainly already waiting in the wings. You just haven't trained yourself to see them there yet. Your team is more than the one friend you trust to cry down the phone to at midnight when your baby can't sleep or your teen hasn't come home yet (although he or she is a really important member). It's more than the one family member who willingly babysits now and again.

Your team is made up of everyone in your network and community who is willing to lend a hand. Including everyone whose job involves doing that too. It's your doctor, your child's teacher, the nursery worker, the librarian, the solicitor, the mum from the parent-teacher association (who you are secretly a little bit scared of on the school run). It's the school counsellor, the local cleaning service, the domestic violence advocate. It's the Facebook friends you only show happy snapshots to right now. It's the people you hide the reality of your struggles from.

It's anyone you become willing to reach out to, with dignity, warmth and honesty, as you grow into the leadership role you now hold.

Your team is built on honesty, humility and courage. Advocacy does not mean you go begging for help or break down because you cannot cope. Advocacy means sharing your vision for the future with people who become inspired to be part of it. It means seeking opportunities and being willing to work hard for them in return.

Advocacy is saying 'I want to start my own business and I need advice on how to arrange my childcare needs.' Or asking what clubs and activities your tear-away 14-year-old son might enjoy locally, because you really want him to find an amazing male role model. It's identifying the gaps in your ideal life and calling in the help that you need from a position of clarity, strength and purpose.

Advocacy is never about crying about how hard it all is, or how hard done by you are. It is not humiliation, weakness or failure.

You should know that no leader does every single job all by themselves. A good leader is willing to have a go, and won't ask others to do things they aren't willing to do themselves. They search out and develop the strengths of others whenever possible. A strong team with a strong leader is made up of many skilled contributors all pulling their weight toward a shared goal or vision for the future. One day your children will be part of this family team. If they are too young to do the heavy lifting today, your job is to find other people who can and will share the load.

Think of someone who inspires you right now. If that person came and asked you for help, how do you think that you might feel? Chances are you'd feel honoured to be given the opportunity and privileged to help them on their way. It's also likely that you would feel ok with saying no, because you respect them and trust they would simply find someone else to fill the gap. This is the vibe you are going for. Assertive, appreciative, independent and capable. When you develop this manner of being, you'll find your vibe attracts your tribe.

CASE STUDY: A SCHOOL STORY

I delivered a series of workshops at a school last year to six amazing single mothers. It was a local school, in a small community. None of the women working with me lived more than a few streets away from the school itself. The school was a positive, outgoing institution with a very go-getter ethos. Celebrating family life was integral to the school community. I walked down corridors lined with posters welcoming all kinds of diverse families into the school.

But after working together once a week for almost six weeks, the women in my group and I had a conversation about confidence which surprised me. One by one, the women admitted that they each had driven to school that morning. Each one had chosen to get into their car to drive mere streets from their front door to the school gates, on a sunny day, rather than walk down the street with their children and risk being seen, or spoken to, by other families on the school run.

As a ripple of recognition moved around the room there was initially laughter, and then a thoughtful silence fell. Each woman realized that she had been hiding from her own community, afraid of judgement, afraid of being seen. Each had become afraid to make small talk with her neighbours. Each one had been judging herself and finding her own life so lacking, she acted as if everyone else must be thinking the same.

And yet, around the table that morning, were five other women who were equally afraid to be seen. Five other families who were hiding from each other. Not one of the women in the room judged the person next to them harshly. But each one judged herself so harshly that she had deliberately cut herself — and her children — off in anticipation of judgements no-one was making but herself.

A pact was soon made among these women to walk to school together. To be the network each one needed, wanted, but had tried so hard to be invisible to.

To grow your network, you only need to think for yourself. Decide for yourself that you are worth being seen. Walk with your head held high, exactly as you are, into the community you belong to. Who knows how many other invisible families will be inspired to start walking with you when you do?

In Your Journal:
Calling In, Pushing Out

Today we are going to examine and map the people who are close to you, and think about who is far away. Becoming consciously aware of your networks and supporters is the first step toward being a capable advocate. Don't worry if you discover there are gaps in your network, or find you feel overcrowded by offers of help you no longer need. Getting clarity about what you need, want and require will equip you to call in resources at the same time as pushing out those who drain your energy.

- Start by drawing a small circle in the centre of your page.
- Add larger circles: imagine drawing a solar system or bullseye target.
- Draw a little stick family in the central circle to represent you and your children — only your immediate family belongs here.
- As you move out into the wider circles, begin mapping your friends, family and other supporters.
- Who is part of your support system?
- Consider what role they play in your network or team.
- Do you need more than one map, for personal and practical support, for example?
- Who is close?
- Who is far away?
- Where are there gaps in the support you would like to see?

The Golden Circle

You and your children inhabit the nucleus of your network. As the rings radiate out from this central circle, the one directly alongside it is called the golden circle. This space is reserved for your closest allies, the people who you trust and can turn to as a chosen wider family.

Choose your golden circle carefully. These people reflect who you are and how you are living your life — who you are being — and show up as the people to whom you feel most aligned. They are also your child's closest pool of influencers.

Give serious consideration to these two questions.
- Are they raising you up?
- Or are they holding you back?

It is not uncommon for my clients to realize when they map their network that the golden circle holds a few people they really would prefer to push out. Perhaps those who have taken on too much responsibility for your family unit, or some who feel entitled to comment on your parenting in an intrusive way. Maybe friendships or relationships you have outgrown. Perhaps some with people who take far more than they give. It could be a friend or a grandparent or even your ex-partner.

If any of your golden circle relationships feel heavy or difficult, you may need to gently step them one (or more) circles further from your heart for now. Boundaries are incredibly important to get right, re-setting them takes time, practice and a willingness to accept that you are allowed to say 'no thanks' as well as 'yes please'. These circles will always be fluid and populating them is a life's work, not just an afternoon. Be patient and compassionate with yourself while you reflect on where your networks are today.

Conversely, some clients realize they have been so protective of their own space, too proud or afraid to ask for help, that their golden circle stands empty of the intimacy and love they ache to feel. If this is you, it may be time to call in more meaningful connections with your friends and community.

A Note On Transitions And Challenges

If you have a specific challenge to overcome right now, such as getting divorced or making legal arrangements for child contact, your golden circle may need to make space for some temporary residents.

Your lawyer, for example, or a therapist working with you or your child. Don't feel anxious if the people you need closest to you today are not friends or family. At the heart of this solar system stand only you and your children. As such, you are the source of gravity. You are in control of who comes close enough to assist you on your way.

Once their role is complete, you can gently push them out just as surely as you pulled them in. Feel confident in knowing that you are the custodian of your personal space. Welcome only those who raise you up, empower and encourage you today. Release with gratitude anyone who no longer serves you or your family.

On Children And Their Networks

As your children grow, they will develop their own networks independent of yours. This is natural and essential for their healthy transition to adulthood. When this happens, it is right and expected that you will move out of their nucleus and into their golden circle.

In your child's golden circle, they may hold people close to them that you have chosen to push way out into the far reaches of your galaxy. In your child's golden circle, you may find yourself positioned next to your ex. Remember that to your child, their other parent is defined by a different and separate relationship from the relationship you have defined with your ex.

It can be emotionally challenging to allow your child to experience and develop closeness with people you have actively worked to push out of your life and network. Bear in mind that while you cannot be your child's only influence, you are a very significant one. Even if your child is exposed to a violent, callous, cruel or unreliable other parent, the foundations you create and the networks your family rely upon have the potential to gift your child with a firm foundation of self-worth.

Self-worth will help your child be resilient and strong in the face of challenges. Self-worth is formed by the 'golden cloud' of beliefs we talked about in Chapter 4. Remember: beliefs are formed by people we know, like, love and trust, by the environments and cultures of our childhood and by our direct life experiences.

Positive beliefs are the gifts of our golden circle. Choose a golden circle for yourself that will envelop your child in this positivity, inclusiveness and sense of trust and belonging. Above and beyond material security, emotional security is your most precious legacy for your child.

What's more, be certain that the effort you put into this step along the journey will pay a dividend of skills in the longer term. It is in developing your own advocacy skills, delegating and partnering with your chosen supporters along the way, that you will set a clear example to your children, to show them how to become artists, leaders and storytellers in their own lives too.

Chapter 7

The grief ribbon

All the art of living lies in a fine mingling of letting go and holding on.
- Havelock Ellis

Once upon a time there was a girl. She lived her whole life waiting for the perfect prince to come and rescue her from her tower. One day, a perfect boy came along. He took her dancing in glass slippers and, as she gazed into his beautiful eyes, they shared a 'true love kiss'. She smiled inside, because she knew this was how they began their 'happily ever after' ...

Except they didn't. He wasn't a prince, she wasn't a princess and, as it turned out, dancing in glass slippers and living in towers were very impractical ideas all round.

If you're disappointed that boy meets girl then leaves, then you've probably been sold a story that doesn't really exist in the real world. If you grew up as I did, in a Western society during the Disney era of the 1970s to 1990s, then I'm willing to bet that the fairy story of true love's kiss is as much a part of your cultural conditioning as it was part of mine.

Which means that waking up without your 'other half', feeling abandoned or rejected by your child's other parent, suffering abuse or emotional neglect at the hands of the person you trusted to be your happy ever after … These kinds of experience are going to trigger grief. Grief that has nothing to do with someone dying, and everything to do with love.

The rollercoaster ride of travelling up and down a grief ribbon can be breathtakingly awful. The only thing I know that makes it worse is when the person who is grieving does not feel entitled to do so. Suppressed grief is about the only thing more painful than expressed grief.

So how do you grieve for someone who isn't dead, who you no longer love and who is demonstrably better for you out of your life? It's not easy to express the deep hurt in your heart when you believe the person who caused it is unworthy of your pain. I have met women who are so angry they reject grief completely, believing that grief somehow dignifies the person who has left. That their grief is something their ex-partner and father of their child does not deserve.

If this is you, be reassured. You are not grieving the man who left your life. You are grieving for the woman you once thought you were going to be.

I discovered I was able to let go of the person my ex had turned into completely, and grieve instead for the person I had imagined him to be. The man I had dreamed of sharing my life with wasn't real any more, nor was the life I thought I was living.

So I grieved for the life I had imagined we would have. For the life I had assumed my children would have. I grieved for all the dreams and plans I had woven around a relationship that could never sustain them. For the career and the home I had lost along the way. I grieved for me.

I grieved for myself, for all the versions of myself I had believed I was going to get the chance to be. As I owned my hurt, my disappointment, my anger, my sadness and my pain, I found a way back into myself that would never have been open to me without a willingness to experience grief.

You are entitled to feel gut-wrenchingly hurt by your loss. Losing the dream of a nuclear family is huge. The promise of a two-parent home is sold to us culturally all the time. If you are a single parent today not by choice, then your dream was not to be here, parenting alone. Whatever your dream was before you had a child, or the dream you were building with the father you created your child with, accepting that it is over is a profound loss.

The agony of knowing you will never walk the path you had once seen in front of you clear as day, is hard to describe. It changes you. The death of a loved one is not the only way you can be bereaved. The death of your dreams is just as life-altering an experience to have.

Finding The Gifts Of Grief

A psychiatrist and pioneer in near-death studies called Elisabeth Kübler-Ross first theorized that there are five stages of grief in her book *On Death and Dying*. This famous work is so often quoted today that many of us are vaguely aware of the 'five stages of grief' as a concept. Until you are pitched into a state of grieving, it's hard truly to understand what those stages are like.

At first, there is shock and fear. Numbness, confusion and blame. The awful thing happens and in that moment it kills your dreams of a together life. Whatever it is that pitches you into a conflict-driven, unpleasant separation, the first reaction is rarely to feel sad. Usually, adrenaline and a sense of life being unreal and awful kicks in first.

When the numbness wears off, it is replaced by a hot wave of anger. Rage, frustration, irritation, embarrassment and shame. This is the reaction of your sympathetic nervous system (SNS), the branch of your brain that deals with extreme threat and stress. This is the fight, flight or freeze reaction that carries with it an energizing burst of activity. This is when you are galvanized to take action — calling friends or your solicitor, or calling your ex himself to give him a piece of your mind. Anger is inwardly focused, but outwardly expressed.

When you are angry, you are consumed with yourself. How you are feeling, how you have been wronged, how you will wreak revenge. The heat of your fury touches everyone and everything around you. For some people, this stage is brief. Others, afraid of letting a dragon out, respond by totally shutting down their anger. If anger does not feel safe, they simply will not allow it to arise. So it stays below the surface, a pit of broiling lava that will not be released willingly, but instead seeps out in violent or tearful explosions that can be neither predicted nor explained. Self-harm. An eating disorder. Compulsive shopping, fucking, fighting. Rage at the children, followed by desperate remorse.

And others are so glad to feel anything at all after the shock has worn off that they take up residence in anger for good. Anger feels active, productive and justifiable to many people. But anger over a long time resets the very wiring inside your brain. It transforms you chemically from someone who was able to feel joy and happiness, into someone whose SNS leaps into action at the slightest trigger. Responding with far too much bark, and an occasional bite, to the smallest provocation.

For a parent of young children, residing in hidden or overt anger is living in the badlands. Small people are endlessly provoking. The hot, angry, hurt temper you unleash cannot foster a sense of safety and security for your dependent children. The badlands must be navigated patiently, purposefully and with great commitment. A skillful navigator will be made when you master your own badlands for good. In travelling out of the badlands, however, you are still only part way through your journey of grief.

On the other side of anger, many slip into despair. As adrenaline subsides, a sense of becoming overwhelmed and helpless can arise in its place. Waking up in a version of your life that you did not expect to be living in, where the edges you carefully built around your dreams have been stripped away by the actions of someone else, is a powerless place to arrive at. Knowing that your anger serves no-one and costs you and your children safety and joy is bad enough, but feeling sapped of all energy, detached and depressed can often be worse.

As the depressed and despondent soul struggles to find her way back to a raft of normality, the ribbon begins to curl upward again. At last, we begin to discover some of the great gifts of embarking upon this voyage of personal vulnerability. Tentatively reaching out to other people, beginning to tell your own story in a new way. Searching for meaning in what has just happened to you and your children by opening a dialogue about what has unfolded in your lives. This is the start of integrating your grief, accepting that it belongs to you, has shaped you, and cannot be undone, unlived or rejected any more.

Speaking your truth allows the first sense of acceptance to flow out of this ribbon of grief. With acceptance of what is, and releasing what once was, the SNS in your brain can finally reset its reactive state. You are moving into the parasympathetic nervous system response, the 'rest and digest' to your fight and flight. It is here, in this state, that you can finally begin truly to mentally and emotionally digest what has unfolded in your life, to take stock of where your re-formed family is finding their feet and to explore with curiosity the options that are opening up for you all.

It is in this space that you become an artist. In these moments, you learn how to turn over broken pieces of your life in your hands with loving awareness. Notice exactly where they have fallen apart, see what is beyond repair and what needs to be reset with intention and compassion and skill. It is now you will begin restoring those pieces with gold.

Your artistry is in your words. In the way you tell your story, in the way you share the meaning you have found. In what you are able to accept willingly and welcome as learning along the way.

In my own life, the gifts were learning how to manage my own life practically and financially for the very first time. I learned that I am more capable than I ever dreamed possible. I learned that I can be a safe harbour and a shelter for the grief and confusion of my sons. I discovered that I am strong. That life goes on, even when it looks nothing like I imagined it would. I learned that my story has life-giving power to inspire and create hope for other people. I found my voice, created a new career, learned how to claim space in the world. I wrote this book.

I am more than the wife and mother I once dreamed I was going to be. I will always be sad that young woman's dream wasn't brought to life. But I cannot be sad about the woman I am today. Today I am proud. Today I am grateful. Today, I am truly alive.

Being Human

And yet, even when you have travelled this ribbon in its entirety, when you have arrived at a place filled with meaning, empowerment and confidence in all that you have become, know that the ribbon is a slippery place to stand. Sometimes, just sometimes, you will slide back, bounce around, fall down and find yourself back in a valley you thought you had climbed out of once and for all.

For me those moments come when I least expect them. Like the day I discovered my ex-husband was expecting a child with the woman he left us for. The news came just weeks after we received our decree absolute. Their engagement followed only 14 days after that momentous day. For me, the contrast of his connection to her, as I held the final notice of our own disconnection, was an exquisite kind of pain.

On Christmas Day that year I woke up with my 3-year-old son and my 18-month-old toddler, without their father. On Christmas Day he asked the woman he betrayed us with to be his wife.

There is no denying that in the months that followed this transition I bounced right back to the beginning of the ribbon. I slipped wordlessly from shock and numbness to rage, to sadness for my children and despair for myself ... back to the struggle for a communion with myself. A conversation with my own heart, my own community, those who could love me back to the life I was building myself.

If you find this happens to you too, the comfort I can offer is that the ribbon is always shorter the second time you ride those waves. You will never be as winded as you were the first time.

The second, the third, the fourth and beyond — it becomes a journey with familiar footsteps. I find I can hold my own hand now when these moments arise. Because I am confident that the grief I have learned to carry lightly belongs to me, for myself. It is not for the loss of my husband. I have come to understand that I deserve to show myself the same tenderness and compassion I would show my best friend if she was hurting in this way. It is my decision to practise self-compassion, self-care and to develop my sense of personal worth which has lightened the burden of grief.

I have learned to carry the grief also because I am still able to love that version of myself. The younger me, the vulnerable me, the pregnant and lonely and frightened me. When events unfold today that touch that hurt part of myself, it is that hurt part of myself that I am holding. The love that I have for myself that I am honouring. The tears I shed are for the young woman who did not deserve to be broken-hearted as the opening chords of her life in motherhood were played.

I hold her gently, and today, I love her back to life myself.

Sharing The Family Grief

One of the great gifts of giving yourself permission to grieve for yourself and for your imagined life is that in doing so you will become able to hold your children's grief as well. Remember Catherine, from the first chapter of this book? Her son's grief and anger shook Catherine right to her very core. Seeing him express with all the embodied physicality of childhood how utterly angry and in pain he was touched the part of Catherine that desperately needed to rage with him. She was not really afraid of her son's anger. Catherine was deeply afraid of her own.

Sidestepping a stage on the grief ribbon is not a sustainable plan. There is a natural order that must be allowed to play out. To release numbness, you must allow yourself next to experience pain. The process of experiencing pain is going to tire you out. In order to climb back from this exhausted state, you will need to reach out for the hands of another. As you steady yourself on a new terra firma, you will necessarily discover a new view.

By denying her own pain and shaming or attempting to shut off her son's pain, Catherine was keeping both herself and her son stuck. There was no path out of this place that could heal them without her first acknowledging and allowing the pain to exist. Catherine had to find her way back into her own body, and let it tremble with fire and fury as well. Declare the searing unfairness of her situation and expose the raw wound to the light. Catherine needed someone she trusted to witness her own pain so that she in turn had the capacity to allow her son the great gift of being witnessed in his pain too.

Your anger is as much a part of you as your laughter is. Your pain is yours just as truly as your hopefulness is. You must allow yourself to be whole in order to heal. There is no part of you more worthy than another part. No part can be more welcome than any other. When you have experienced a deep rejection

— and, crucially, when your child has experienced a deep rejection — you cannot heal it by further rejecting those angry, afraid and vulnerable parts of yourself or your child that need to be held.

Healing will come when you hold space for these parts of you and your child to exist. Your home can be a place where all of you is welcome. All of you is loved. All of you belong.

Becoming A Harbour

Becoming a harbour means becoming a place where your child is welcome. A space that contains and keeps them safe. It means meeting your child's anger, grief or depression with the sure knowledge that as they are, you are. As you are, so are they.

There is nothing your child can feel that you do not. Nothing your child can express that you cannot feel. Empathy is the oil that stills troubled waters. The most powerful thing you can give an angry child is validation. Know that when you offer this, it is costing you nothing at all. Accepting that your child has the right to feel what they feel is only accepting their right to be human. Remind yourself that they are no more or less human than you are.

If their anger makes you angry, you are normal. If their grief hurts you desperately, you are touching the depths of your love for one another. If their sadness makes you cry, feel blessed for the gifts of connection that these experiences offer you both.

It makes sense that they would feel this way.

It makes sense that you would feel this way.

Together, you will make sense of your world.

IN YOUR JOURNAL: EXPLORING FAMILY GRIEF

Take some time to explore your own feelings of grief and loss, and to reflect on how your children may be experiencing grief. While it may be difficult to invite these feelings in, welcoming them will begin to soften their impact.

- What is my child's pain reflecting to me that I reject in myself?
- What would it feel like to accept the hurt and angry parts of me so that I can accept the hurt and angry parts of my child?
- How is my fear of witnessing their feelings creating a fear-based relationship between us?
- What will it take to centre myself enough to be still in the face of their pain?

What can grief look like in children?

0–2

- feeding and sleeping difficulties
- regressive behaviour (thumb sucking, losing interest or ability to be potty trained, clingy)
- intense separation anxiety and fear of abandonment

2–5

- sleep problems, fear of the dark, unable to self-settle
- angry and defiant about changes to their daily routine
- anxiety, fear that they are the cause of the separation or a problem for their parents
- tummy aches, vomiting, headaches
- toileting problems
- regressive behaviour (thumb sucking, bed-wetting, clingy)
- withdrawn or explosive, difficulties regulating their own emotions, hits out at other children

4–11

- withdrawn, sad or lonely
- difficulty concentrating
- unpredictable temper tantrums, angry outbursts
- tries to be 'perfect' and feels panic or despair if chastised

- tries to control things (food, their environment, peers, games)
- regressive behaviour (thumb sucking, bed-wetting, clingy)
- blames others for how they feel ('You made me angry')
- struggles to express verbally how they feel.

If you think your child is struggling with grief and this is being reflected in their behaviour, remember you do not have to deal with it on your own. Put on your advocacy hat and grow your network. Call in the team that you need with confidence and authority — your family is not the first to struggle with this issue and your children will not be the last. Asking for help does not mean you are a bad parent or that you have let them down so far. Asking for help is the mark of a strong and compassionate leader at work.

- Who can help me support my child?
- Who can help me resource myself?
- Where can I find the information I need to be able to cope?
- What do we need as a family to help us grieve?

Chapter 8

A learning experience

....

It's not that I'm so smart.
But I stay with the questions much longer.
Albert Einstein

....

The upward curls of acceptance, empowerment and purpose lift each of us out of the
trenches each in our own particular way. The
place upon which we find ourselves standing at the
end of this journey is like a mountain top. For the
first time, we are able to stand on our story, and not
in it. The meaning you find in where you have been
transforms trauma from an identity you wear day and
night, into a learning experience you can separate
yourself from, observe and set aside. It will always be
significant, part of the many experiences that have
shaped who you are, but it is no longer the one that
defines you.

At the top of this mountain you are given an
opportunity to take in the breathtaking view. Laid
out below you is the path you took to arrive here. For

the first time since you began the climb, you are also in a position to choose with clarity the path that will take you on from here.

The quality of self-leadership you are called to develop at this point in your life, both as a woman and a mother, is no more and no less than the attitude that you are capable of growth. On the surface of it, this is a simple thing to do. But in reality, a positive growth mindset is one of the most challenging and rewarding things you can consciously develop. A growth mindset means finding evidence that you are learning in the experiences you have that do not go well. Both in the past and future.

Finding meaning in any single traumatic event or experience has been an epic journey of self-discovery so far. You have come an extraordinary distance already if you have worked through the steps in this book. In the quest for a meaningful or purposeful life, this new skill must be nurtured and honoured in you. As a parent, the great gift of committing to a growth mindset will be helping to shape your children's emerging rule book for life. The empowering beliefs that will carry them forward on a golden cloud of positivity, out of childhood into adulthood, with confidence, courage and a deep sense of inner calm.

A growth mindset will challenge you to see each setback from now on as a simple step on a learning journey. There is no place for blame or shame or self-loathing in a family vision built on a willingness to try.

Relationships are always a vehicle for learning. They show up and reflect back to us parts of ourselves, inviting us to become aware of them. The one that ended with your ex invited you to strengthen your boundaries, discover your personal values and make a decision to stand up for yourself with true integrity today. For all it cost you, the journey has offered you something of value in return. The brave and compassionate woman you are today can accept this learning knowing full well that accepting a positive out of a negative does not mean you must accept the negative.

Looking for the learning does not mean letting the person who wronged you off the hook. Gratitude for all you have discovered about who you are and how your life can expand at this point is not gratitude for being hurt in the first place. Your gratitude, just like your grief, is first and foremost toward yourself — what an incredible woman you are! Incredible for having lived through this troubling time and arrived at the top of your own personal mountain, not only stronger, wiser and braver — but holding the hands of your children and showing them the way too.

I am unfailingly impressed when I work with parents like you and witness this moment of recognition. To me, it's like graduating from the university of life. Perhaps you won't be handed an actual diploma to mount on your wall, but the up-levelling of your internal state is no less worthy of recognition than if you had been granted a master's degree. Here you are, having worked your butt off to assimilate all this learning. Now just as with a master's degree, you are about to see how it works when you apply your learning in the world.

The truth is, in practice, it's not always as straightforward as it might look on a page. So this chapter should be the one that you bookmark and come back to, time and again. When you feel unsettled or worse, knocked down by life again — pick this book up and check this chapter again. These are the core questions to ask yourself every time you feel you are taking a step backward instead of forward.

- What could you try?
- What have you learned?
- Where can you go next?
- Who can help you with this?
- What worked before?
- What might work now?
- How has getting this wrong helped you figure out something important?

- What are your priorities now?
- What is this situation reminding you of?
- Are your reactions based on feelings or on facts?
- How will trying again get you where you want to be?
- How could walking away get you where you want to be?
- What will help you make the decision?

CASE STUDY: JENNY'S STORY

Jenny had two children with complicated additional needs. Simply showing up to work with me was a challenge, something that many parents will be unable to understand. It required a level of organization and dedication that went beyond just making some time for herself. Carving out the emotional energy required and protecting her right to claim this back for herself was immensely important. It was humbling to walk with Jenny as she reclaimed her right to an independent life.

At twelve and fourteen, her girls were not much less demanding than children ten years younger might have been, although differently so. Their father had lived at home for the majority of their childhood, inflicting mental and emotional abuse on Jenny, before eventually abandoning them as they reached the cusp of adolescence. A decade of parenting them largely alone had left Jenny exhausted and raw. However, she had no desire to share parenting, and was not seeking respite or relief from her children.

Jenny wanted respite from the internal war she had waged upon herself for so long — the war in her head that insisted she was not good enough. That she was not enough, full stop. Despite fighting an internal, silent battle that had almost defeated her, Jenny was determined not to succumb.

At the top of her personal mountain, Jenny realized she could stand with her back to the sun setting on the path she had climbed to get here, and face forward toward the bright stars in her night sky. She could choose the stars that would become her constant companion and guide her through the days to come. And from this place, Jenny confided in me that she felt like a new era was about to begin.

An era where taking responsibility for herself and her children would include allowing others to share the journey with them. Jenny shared how she had realized her role was bigger than being their mother. It was also to be their role model, their advocate and their guide. Intertwined with her aspiration for her girls to have an independent and fulfilling life would be her own example of achieving this. Nothing would inspire or encourage them to reach for their own potential more than witnessing her reach for her own.

And even if they would never lead independent lives, never be able to achieve what their mother was able to achieve, Jenny allowed herself to believe she still had a right to life.

There is no circumstance, no challenge, no relationship or limitation that will remove your right to a life of your own.

The realization that Jenny must claim her right to life and act upon it was profound. From this place, Jenny found she could expand the edges of her world exponentially. Far beyond where I or any of her friends or supporters up until now had been able to imagine for her. With the deep inhale of possibility and exhale of acceptance, Jenny began to design a beautiful, courageous new life.

IN YOUR JOURNAL:
ENTITLED TO LEARN

When we began this journey together, I asked you to think about the assumptions and expectations you held about 'people like me' and 'people like them'. Now, I invite you to push hard against the boundaries of these ideas.

- Who is like you, really?
- Who has a life just like yours?
- Who can stand in your shoes and know just what it's like to walk a mile in them?
- Is there anyone who has the same potential, opportunities or learning journey to travel as you?

In reality we are completely and totally unique. There will always be similarities with others. The call to find your tribe, to belong, to conform, is so deeply rooted in our ancestral DNA that none of us can be immune to the call for companionship. But just as each of the stories my clients have shared in this book will speak to something you can relate to, each one will show you how different we all are as well. Mothers who are parenting alone, yes, but also women who are learning to claim their authority, agency and right to their own fulfilling lives.

You can find companionship today without conforming to another person's expectations. To be immune to others' expectations, however, you must take responsibility for yourself. The first thing you are going to have to do is to honestly examine your own expectations.

Just like in Chapter 4, when we worked our way through the mechanics of our beliefs, I'd like you to reflect on your expectations of life as they are today.

IN YOUR JOURNAL: MY EXPECTATIONS UNCOVERED

Set aside half an hour. Make sure this is time by yourself in a nurturing and calm environment. This must be a safe space for your unconscious self to speak your truth.

Writing as a stream of consciousness means that you begin writing on a topic, and simply continue until you run out of words completely. As you are writing, do not self-censor, edit, read back, correct your own grammar or spelling. Simply continue forward, noticing without judgement the words that arise. They will tell you so much about your onward journey and what it has in store.

Begin with these statements, and for each one, take a new page, a new stream of consciousness, and simply write. Be mindful that the statement is not what you hope or dream or aspire for, but what you expect. The part of you that answers when you allow it to, unchallenged, will be more truthful than the part that wants to sound good. Allow whatever your unspoken self wants to say to be welcome.

* I expect that I will …
* I expect my son(s) will …
* I expect my daughter(s) will …
* I expect my family and friends will…
* I expect my future or current lover will…
* I expect that men in my life will…

When you are done, relax and give yourself some loving kindness. Accepting and welcoming all of your thoughts, both the happy and sad, the anxious and excited, is all about welcoming yourself. Reclaiming your one wonderful, extraordinary life as your own.

After a time, go back and read what your soul spoke into these pages. Take two coloured pens with you when you do.

> Highlight the expectations that fill you with joy and positivity. Highlight also those that bring up worry, sadness or fear.

Here the onward journey is about to begin. Confronting those fears will become a life's work. A journey of learning like no other you have been on before. You will be walking in community with yourself from here on in — holding each part of you with a commitment that you are welcome.

As you are, so is everyone else. As everyone else is, so are you.

Each of you is uniquely made and yet part of the world at large. Neither alone nor entwined with any other soul.

It's time to create your vision.

Chapter 9

Drafting a vision for family life

....

Absorbed in this world, you've made it your
burden.
Rise above this world.
There is another vision.
All your life you've paid attention to your
experiences, but never to your Self.
Are you searching for your Soul?
Then come out of your prison. Leave the stream
and join the river that flows into the Ocean.
It will not lead you astray.
Let the beauty you seek be what you do.
Rumi

....

We are finally at the threshold of designing your new life. This chapter is dedicated to exploring the purpose of your vision, but also to the practice of creating one for yourself. I will show you exactly how to take the learning you have gained from the pages of your journal and turn it into a cohesive map that will guide you through your life as it unfolds from here.

Let The Beauty You Seek Be What You Do

Returning to the first question in this book is the foundation of your family vision: Who are you being today? This is the essence of vision-building for your family. The very first concept to grasp is that a vision does not only refer to the distant future. It begins right here, right now, in the day you are in, with the way you are acting, in the here and now. The beauty you seek in your future has already begun to unfold. It is germinating in who you are being today, as you put pen to paper and craft your vision for life.

Just as your values are not destinations, understand that your vision is not a series of fixed points along a predetermined road ahead. You may well have markers of success along the way — being free from debt, or reaching a business milestone, relocating into your dream house for example. You may date stamp these markers — five years or eight years or ten years from today. These are all important and motivating things to include in your overall vision for life.

The essence of your vision however is to already be the things you want your family to become. So in my family vision, with our astral navigation points of 'kindness' 'bravery' 'adventure' and 'fun', the vision for our future is itself made up of many individual golden threads, held together with these principles as the glue.

In action, this is what it looks like. When I make a decision about anything significant for myself and my children, such as where we will live, how I will work, what I will invest in my children's future, the kind, brave, adventurous and fun version of myself is called forward every step of the way. I want to be sure that when I meet the woman I will become in five, ten, fifteen years from now, she will thank the version of me as I am today for helping her become as kind, brave, adventurous and fun as she is.

Even more than that, I want to be sure that the grown men I send out from my lap into the world are men that are kind, brave, adventurous and fun.

Helping each of us to grow into this version of ourselves in the crucible of our healed family and home is the mission that my vision will carry. Getting the detail right is very important.

IN YOUR JOURNAL:
MOVING FROM DREAMS TO DETAILS

Vision-building is more than just having some guiding principles in mind. While your family values are profound and important, and yours will matter to you just as much as mine do to me, values alone do not make a vision. A vision is something more than that.

A vision is a picture of your life brought to life with your emotions, your energy and your absolute commitment to seeing it through.

Beginning with one single question today, I would like you to begin to record the detailed answers to what a life well lived means to you. Take some time, without self-censorship and on a clean page, and write everything that comes to mind from this one question.

- What do you want your children to know about themselves, about the world and about you when they are grown and leaving home?

When you run out of answers take stock. After some time, read back over what you have written and work your way through each of these developmental questions.

From inside this core question we discover that there are many, many more that unfold.

- How will they learn this about themselves?
- How will they learn this about the world?
- How will they know this about you?
- Who do you have to be today for your children to experience life this way?
- What do you need to learn, try, change or do differently today to make this vision come to life?

As you sit with these questions, give yourself plenty of time, space and creative opportunity to record your ideas. Some people like using their journal, others like to mind map on a large piece of paper. I am the doodling and drawing kind — I usually grab a piece of A3 or A2 card and work my way around all the areas of my life with each of these questions in mind.

The areas I encourage you to examine in depth include:

- your professional life, working hours, aspirations and work–life balance
- your relationship with your children
- your relationships with your significant other (or imagined future partner)
- your relationships with your extended family, with your friends, your role in your community
- your home environment
- your childcare choices
- your education and your children's education
- your personal development and your children's development
- your holidays, down time, activities and treats
- your diet, health and exercise
- your children's relationship with their father, wider family and connections outside of you and yours.

This can seem like a daunting task. It is not a one-stop shop activity. You can expect your vision to take several weeks to draft in full. When I work with clients, we usually allow between three and four weeks of sustained effort to complete this draft. The outcome is worth every effort you put in. With your guiding principles at the heart of everything you capture, record the best version of your family's lives that you can imagine in all of these areas.

A peaceful job role, peaceful relationships, peaceful home, peaceful opportunities to learn and grow, peaceful places to rest and relax and explore, a peaceful relationship with yourself and your body, a peaceful relationship with the father of your child.

A brave career, brave relationships, brave choices at home, brave risks in learning, growing and challenging yourselves, brave holidays and activities, brave commitment to health and wellbeing, brave resolutions to the on-going challenge of continuing (or ending) your child's relationship with their father.

A career to be proud of, relationships you are proud of, achievements you are proud of to better yourselves, pride in your home and your gifts to yourself of relaxation, fun and adventure. Pride in your health and appearance. Pride in yourself and a dignified relationship with your ex and wider family wherever possible.

Can you see how each of these principles conjure up a completely different picture in your mind? Explore yours patiently, with commitment and systematically. Do not skip over areas that feel challenging or unsettling. Apply the same basic method every time.

- In each area of your life, with your values as the guiding principle, what does alignment look like?

Each vision drawn up by the loving and courageous leader of a family is unique. Each one I have had the privilege to witness is rich with potential. Possibilities come alive and are made significant with the commitment to detail.

When you dedicate yourself to this process and take the time needed to connect emotionally as well as intellectually with your vision, it becomes possible to almost see, touch, taste and smell the experiences you want to bring to life. I encourage you to do so! Find the most vivid and sensory-rich ways possible to feel your way into this life. The more emotionally connected you become to your best imagined life, the more real, achievable and necessary it will be for you to create it.

Your vision must reach a place where it slips from a draft, doodle and dream into a necessary, vivid and compelling reality that you clearly see is within your reach. It is from this place that all your choices will begin to fall into alignment in order to make this vision come true.

You will no longer see your values as options. They will become a way of being. No longer the 'wouldn't that be nice' life, but the 'come what may' life you are committed to having.

Your vision will become compelling, meaningful and motivating. Steven Covey used these words when describing the process of creating a vision in his book *The Seven Habits of Highly Effective Families*. They are incredibly important words to sit with now. Here they are:

- compelling
- meaningful
- motivating.

Does your vision, as you have drafted it today, give you such a profound sense of meaning that you feel compelled to see it through? Will coming back to this vision for your life and your children's lives breathe enough energy into your being that you will work evenings, weekends, nap times, through emotional, physical, mental and practical challenges, to make it happen? Do you care deeply, sincerely, unquestioningly, about the life you have described so far?

This is your own, extraordinary, unique and wonderful life.

- What are you going to do with it?
- What are you going to create with it?
- How are you going to honour it?
- What gifts are you giving your children through their experience of growing up with you?

You are a powerful artist, visionary and authority in your home now. The vision you create is the glue that will reset every broken piece of the life you had before and restore the vessel of your family to a purposeful and useful state.

A family is a vessel for everyone it contains. It both holds each of you and receives each of you, just as you are. Inside the unified, unbroken, gilt-seamed and shining vessel you are creating now, both you and your children will be carried through life, safe, supported and secure.

The detail of your vision that will hold, contain, soothe and support each of you is found in how you set your intentions from this day forward. No matter what car you drive, what house you live in, what income you have, make a decision that your heart will be peaceful, kind, courageous or gentle — starting now, today, where you are. No matter how your child comes to you, be it anxious, grieving, mischievous, wild, hurting or exuberant, understand that how your heart receives them from now on will set the tone for your shared lives to come.

You do not need anything material. You do not already have to begin living life in line with your vision today. Every step you take and brick you make with your clear and committed intentions will build around you the material life you hope to see. It is your intention, attitude and motivation to live with aligned values that calls material success toward you. Striving for material success alone will not bring you peace and joy.

Begin With The End In Mind

I have found little more compelling than imagining the grown men and women you have raised acting in the world with the integrity, compassion, purpose and confidence that you gifted to them in their childhood.

Successful and happy men and women who have good relationships and make a positive impact in the world do not have perfect lives without challenge or heartbreak along the way. However, they do have one thing in common. They learned either as children, or as you are now, in later life, that happiness and success is about choosing to be the best version of yourself in the here and now. Finding the evidence all around you that you are capable and life is ultimately good, even when you're walking through a dark night of your soul. In knowing that the answer is simply to keep walking, because dawn will surely come.

Lift your eyes to your own horizon now. The days of the trenches are far, far behind you.

Part Three

Closing the Circle

....

As a leader, it's a major responsibility on your shoulders to practice the behaviour you want others to follow.
Himanshu Bhatia, founder and CEO, Rose International

....

Your vision is a beautiful, complex thing once it is complete. Finally you have drawn for yourself the details, contours, obstacles and pathways on the map we first unfolded together in Part One. You have now plotted both point A and point B. The various routes you can travel between the two are sketched on to the page and all that remains is to begin taking steady steps forward.

Armed as you now are, with your own internal compass and a set of navigation skills, you no longer need me to hold the map for you. It can feel scary to wave goodbye to the guide you leaned upon up till now and trust that you know enough to travel safely on alone. Remember that fear is a travelling companion to all of us. You will do well to make friends with fear — just don't give fear the keys to drive your car or allow it to set your course. Fear hasn't got the skill set you have worked so hard to develop, and more often than not drives in reverse.

Keep your momentum going by sharing what you have learned. The best way to hold on to our skills when we become independent travellers is to give them away to other people we meet along the way. Practise what you have learned in this book. If you meet someone who looks lost, practise holding their map for them rather than telling them where to go. Watch them learn to navigate for themselves. Remember that we are all on a journey so unique that advice and direction more often than not throws us off course. Recall how I met you exactly where you were in Chapter 1, inviting you to consider who you were being. I believed in your competence to do this work no matter where you were starting your journey from. Remember how it felt to have someone believe in you until you were able to trust yourself again. In return, I ask you to commit to trusting others. Gift them with the enormously powerful experience of being allowed to think for themselves.

Do this especially for your children as they grow. Hold out their maps, remind yourself how you learned to navigate and become a teacher where once you were a student. Your students will teach you far more than you ever expected they could. In this way, we become more than the parents who stayed to raise our children. We are a movement of families raising a generation of children governed by their values, contributing their best selves to the world.

Chapter 10

The female CEO (being a boss at home)

....

Leadership is about making others better as a result of your presence and making sure that impact lasts in your absence.
Sheryl Sandberg, Facebook CEO and single parent

....

Congratulations on reaching this milestone in your journey as a lone parent. You have come a long, long way from the woman who was just about holding it all together. With a clear vision for the future you now want to create for your family, you are standing at the threshold to a completely new life.

Here on this threshold, while it may be thrilling, you will surely find the first of many obstacles in your way. I say this not to suck your courage back out from underneath you, but because honesty is important. If a vision alone were enough to change the world, we'd all be pasting pictures on to vision boards willy-nilly and placing our orders to the universe on a nightly basis. In reality, once you climb that mountain, turn your back on the path you took to reach the summit, and face the new dawn ahead, the only way forward is to take a step back off that vantage point, and descend in a new direction.

Once you move off the mountain top, you will of course become immersed in your journey again. With luck, the route forward you choose will lead you into lush valleys and temperate climates. Life is often a curious blend of luck and challenge, however. So, it's to be expected that you will occasionally be thrown off course. Your ability to navigate by your own guiding stars is going to be tested all the time, and sometimes you will make mistakes. If you wake up one morning and realize you are nowhere near where you set out to be, stay calm. A series of small adjustments to your course will bring you back to the centre path again.

Why Here? Why Now?

There will be many times you are called to question your decisions and doubt your capacity to guide your family onward. If you never had self-doubt, courage would quickly become foolishness. Doubt keeps you questioning, learning and growing, as long as you use it as an opportunity to check yourself, and not as an excuse to stop yourself.

There will always be reasons to doubt, worry or fret. Never let your reasons become excuses. The only failure that truly comes from a mistake is when you do not learn from it.

There will never be a time more appropriate or more significant to undertake this work on yourself than right now. This is because the only time anything is guaranteed to you, is here, now, in this moment. Yesterday is gone, and tomorrow isn't promised, so be willing to start where you are, use what you have in front of you and simply do what you can. Every action taken from this place will yield results.

The world is crying out for better leadership right now. Across our communities, nations, global humanity, there is a desperate need for people to step up and contribute a new kind of leadership based on integrity, personal awareness and compassionate action. If you and I step back and wait for someone else to step forward, we may be waiting a very long time. Remember the problems we examined right at the start of this book?

Changing and controlling others is not an option available to any person alive today. We have neither the ability nor the right to force other people to behave the way we would wish them to. Each of us is a universe unto ourselves — our power and our responsibilities lie in changing and controlling our own actions and reactions. When the scale of the global problem seems too vast to contemplate, begin with what is simply here in front of you. Stop looking outside of your front door for a solution. Close it firmly and do the work you can on improving life inside your own home.

What you nurture in your own home, within your own hearts will walk out of your front door to make an impact in your neighbourhood, your wider community and family, your society at large and, ultimately, will contribute to the world as we know it. What happens inside your front door is as significant as throwing the proverbial pebble in a pond. Cast your stone with intention, and watch those ripples move far beyond the reach you once thought you had.

Leadership Begins At Home

What will it cost you and your family not to do this now? It is hard to say exactly what living without vision may cost you and your children going forward from here. But I know with certainty that my clients can usually identify what it has cost them up until now. Not knowing who you are, what you stand for, what you will protect, defend and nurture; the absence of these things has paved the way for being abused, hurt, disappointed and cowed by relationships and life.

You may have once known yourself better than you did when your relationship ended and you picked up this book. But if you felt that you lost yourself, sacrificed yourself or emptied yourself of these things in order to keep someone else happy, you will know in a resonant way what your lack of vision has cost you already. Right here, and right now, you can make a decision to prevent this from happening to you again.

Knowing who you are will allow you to develop the strong boundaries that will keep you safe and make you and your children strong. You will discover that self-respect means saying no. Respecting others also means saying no. When you state what is and is not ok with you with clarity and kindness, it does not limit your life, rather it expands it exponentially. 'No' will give you the freedom to make room for the resounding 'yes' that comes with a good decision made from a respectful, self-aware and confident place.

When you think back to the moments of despair and loneliness you have experienced so far, you will see how valuable the belonging and togetherness of a unified family vision will be to you and your children as you grow.

I recall vividly sitting on the top step, by the landing outside my toddler's bedroom, weeping with exhaustion as he tried to climb out of his bed yet again. I had been on my own nearly a year. Feeling so utterly alone in that moment, without direction, purpose or connection to the life I found myself in. The crushing feeling of being alone fed into my own fears of being adrift in life. In turn cutting me off from soothing and connecting with my children. Stripping me of the energy I needed to cope with the realities of parenting young children alone.

I needed to know where I was going in order to pick us all up and set off in that direction with gusto. The vision I created did not simply perk me up when I had time to think about five, eight or ten years down the line. The vision gave me a framework to take on the relentless sleep deprivation, financial challenge and organizational chaos of starting my life over again.

I understand that it takes time to stop crying on the stairs and tune in to the bigger picture. But with your growing self-awareness will come confidence, perspective and connection. Your mental health will improve. You will rely less on quick fixes and instant gratification to feel better about life. The call of social media or shopping or that cool glass of wine at the end of another stressful day will begin to fade.

The hard graft of raising your growing children will once again fall into its proper perspective. With each challenging phase (I have yet to meet an unchallenging phase), you will discover new ways to guide, develop and respond to your children in line with the life you are designing for them.

You are responsible for and capable of shaping your child's world view, belief system and expectations of life. They will become the kind of person you show them how to be. While this may sound intense or overwhelming at first, it is simply a reversal of the fear so many parents in a high-conflict situation arrive with when I meet them. The fear that the parent who left will have damaged, influenced or harmed their child irrevocably drives so many of my clients to try and control the people or world their child is in contact with. Turn this around now and choose to celebrate how much influence you have, simply with your presence, to counter the negativity your children may have witnessed so far.

Own your capacity to be the change that makes it ok for them. Your ability to show your children intimacy, integrity and self-leadership is the best way to protect them from experiencing unhealthy relationships of their own in their future. Through their experience of being loved, cared for and responded to by you, they will learn how to expect love to feel.

Make it feel good. Make it feel challenging, nurturing, respectful, generous and kind. Love your children the way you want the world at large to love them. The way you want them to love the people they meet. You are so powerful in this moment. Your love can still the ocean itself if you let it.

Love does not conquer all in a pragmatic sense. Love will not prevent poverty or ill health or calamity from occurring. But love will make it possible to live through any of these with the potential for joy to coexist. You have this potential inside you, all the time.

Love yourself with the fierceness with which you love your children. Love yourself with the commitment, honour and passion that you desire from a partner one day. The relationship you have with yourself will set the tone for every new relationship you develop hereafter, so let it be a love affair. Wild, exhilarating and free — everything your previous relationship failed to be. You hold the keys to your happiness in your own hands already. Do not give them to anyone unworthy of you ever again.

Chapter 11

Living with love

Love yourself first and everything else falls into line. You really have to love yourself to get anything done in this world.
Lucille Ball

What will this process give your family? The benefits of living with vision, implemented with love, are really quite significant. From the positive impact on your personal mental health and wellbeing, to the development of a series of key skills in your family, you will begin to see measurable progress toward a better life.

The core skills you develop on your vision-building journey will be passed on to your children as you put them into practice.

Listening To Understand Not To Instruct

Learning to listen to yourself and tune into your intuition is difficult. As you practise the core skill of paying attention to the small voice inside yourself that knows where to go, the voice of your own internal navigator, you will develop a level of confidence you may never have experienced before. Gifting your children with this ability to tune in to themselves is one of the most protective and powerful things you can do as a parent.

The way to help them develop their intuition is to show them that their internal voice matters and will be listened to. When challenges arise in their lives, practise listening in to this internal navigator together.

Especially as they grow toward adolescence, engage them in conversations about how they make decisions.

You could ask them these questions.

- What does your inner voice want to do?
- How do you feel when you act this way?
- What feels like a good decision?
- How does it feel when you mess up?
- How do you decide when to trust yourself?
- How do you know when you get it right?

Share with your children how it feels to you when you make a good decision. Talk to them about how you tune into your intuition, and have conversations right from the get go about where feelings live inside your bodies. Even a three-year-old can begin to think about feelings and their body. At any point from this age on, you can begin.

Ask them to focus on their feelings.

- Is it prickly?
- Is it big?
- Is it heavy?
- Is it fleeting?
- Does it move around?
- Where is it right now?
- Does anxiety live in your stomach?
- In your throat?
- Or somewhere else?
- How about anger, or sadness or fear?

Name and locate feelings that guide you. Help your child to do the same. Every time you work on this skill together you are equipping them to make difficult decisions confidently, without relying on someone else's judgement to tell them if it's ok. As much as we may want to direct our children in their choices, long term we want them to make good ones all by themselves. Under the tutelage of a calm, loving, visionary parent, they will learn more about how to make good choices than an obedient child who follows directions ever could.

Obedient children are susceptible to peer pressure, the dominant influence of a future partner, teacher, boss or friend. Each time you face defiance, try to welcome it internally (even if you do not manage to do so externally!). This is your child honing their self-protection skills. To defend against abuse, injustice and oppression, this reaction needs to be skillfully educated — not squashed. It's hard, but your patience today will protect your child from more of what you've experienced together in the past. Take a deep breath and take the long view.

Your vision no doubt includes raising children who know how to have healthy, respectful relationships. So, while their internal defences need a voice, they also need discipline. To know when it's appropriate to gather up arms, and when to stand down the little warrior inside. You are the one who can help set their emotional thermostat back to normal.

Hypervigilance, sensitivity and fear are the result of living with conflict. They set a child up to live in their fight, flight and freeze state. If your child is in this place, understand that they got this way because, up until now, it helped to keep them safe — to them, it makes sense to react this way. You may also have been living on a short fuse for some time. To you, it has made sense to be reactive too. Gently responding to fear and frustration over time will show all of you that you are safe, without the need to protect yourselves further from hurt. Consistent, patient boundaries will help all of you scale down your response.

Making Choices Together And Being Allowed To Fail

It follows on from learning how to make good choices that occasionally you and your children will mess up. No-one is perfectly successful when learning a new skill. It takes practice to figure out what it feels like to make a good choice, free from influence, obligation or social conditioning. You won't always nail it and neither will they.

Be compassionate with each other as you grow together. Meet failure and disappointment with kindness. Lean into why the outcome feels bad.

- What have you learned?
- What will you try and do differently next time?
- How will this experience help each of you listen to your navigator better?

Failure is only a step on your learning journey. The growth mentality that will help each of you hone your skills is already there — you were born with it. Watch (or remember) your baby become a toddler, then your toddler become a child. They literally stumble and fall over, and they do it over and over again. But each time they get frustrated, notice how they look carefully at your reaction and choose whether it's ok or safe to try again now. Make it safe for your children to try again when they mess up as they get older. Show them that you give yourself permission to mess up too.

This doesn't mean hiding or glossing over mistakes. On the contrary, it means opening up a space where it's safe to talk about what went wrong.

- Where did you go off course?
- How do you know?
- Can you pinpoint that feeling in your body?
- What would help you tune into feeling like that in the future?
- Can you find another similar feeling, one that was warning you to stop before you messed up and got left with the regretful feeling you have now?

These negative experiences are helping you each become skilled at navigating your life. Embracing them will give both you and your children a foundation of loving self-acceptance, along with the capacity lovingly to accept the limitations and mistakes of others.

With the ability to accept each other comes love. With a willingness to examine respectfully your own part in mistakes comes growth, and the capacity not just to love, but to relate to another person in healthy ways. In my own and my clients' lives, there is rarely a skill we crave more than the ability to love and relate with self-respect and respect for others. You can learn how to do this today, and so can your child. However bad your break-up has been. However damaged you feel you and your children have been by what has passed, know that it has passed. The rebuilding of your capacity to love is beginning now.

Communication That Unlocks The Team Mentality

We are neither superior nor inferior to any other person. In a family, we may have more responsibility for others when we are the parent. However, this does not mean that our responsibility makes our needs either more, or less, important than those of our children.

Communicating a vision to your children means holding their wants, needs and wishes in mind when you pursue the goals you have. Leadership means listening deeply to those you wish to bring with you when you set the course. Knowing how they really feel, what truly matters to them. This knowledge will help you to understand why, both when they agree and when they disagree with you. If you can understand your children, their motivations, fears and dreams, you have much more chance of keeping them with you when your vision means making hard choices, sacrifices or changes to your routine, lifestyle and expectations.

Each of you will have your own manner and reactions to challenge. Your children may respond very differently to stress than you do. Bear in mind that a child who has been living in a stressful home will be predisposed to being very sensitive and remain that way for some time after the stress has subsided. This can come out in explosive temper tantrums, inexplicable anxiety attacks or a lack of awareness of risk. You may also see regression to more childish behaviours such as bed-wetting, separation anxiety and food or toileting problems.

As frustrating and upsetting as some of these can be, remember before you see a behaviour, there is always a feeling first. Learn to listen deeply to the feeling this behaviour is expressing, then teach your child in turn to listen to what they are feeling. With understanding comes calm.

Nothing settles and soothes a person more than feeling understood by the people on whom they most need to rely. This is true for adults as well as children. Even if it doesn't make sense to you yet, bear in mind that however your child is feeling, it makes sense to them that they feel this way. Find out why and you will be showing them the respect and connection than builds epic teamwork.

People who feel connected, understood, supported, seen and loved for who they are are inevitably invested in the people who make them feel that way. It is when we are disconnected, misunderstood, unseen and feel unloved that we check out of our family life.

There is no challenging behaviour that does not change with love and understanding. Just as there is no vision you can communicate without learning to listen to your children and yourself first. Do the work on yourself first, then lay solid foundations with each person in your home. The vision will unfold from there.

Delegating Responsibilities To Nurture Skills And Self-Esteem

Give up a little control over how you arrive where you're planning on going. It's really, really hard to let go of wanting to be in charge of every step of the journey. Especially when the path it took to get here has been peppered with chaos, upheaval, unhappiness or stress. I know it's hard to let go. But let go, and you will see great leaps in learning, motivation and skill all around you.

Sometimes being a good leader means allowing other people to shine. The more responsibility you give your kids as they grow, the more they will be able to grow into the responsibility over time. Maybe they won't do things the way you would prefer, or they may choose a different path than the one to which you would have directed them. But if they figure challenges out for themselves, then you might just get more than you bargained for in wonderful ways. If you nurtured their internal navigators, the natural result is that you will be able to trust them to behave with integrity toward themselves as adults.

So, teach the values you most want your children to know and teach them to tune into how it feels to navigate by these points. Then sit back and let them do it for themselves. Watch the magic unfold as the vision you had for yourself and your children grows exponentially with the input of your children over time. Together you will achieve so much more!

Guiding And Working With Natural Personality Traits (Yours And Theirs)

Back in the beginning we looked at how seeing characteristics of your ex-partner brought to life in your children as they grow can act as a trigger. The raw materials each of us are born with can be nurtured and guided, but not changed. We are gifted with the temperaments of our ancestors, as well as the attitudes of our time.

Practise noticing the raw material your child is manifesting without ascribing a meaning to it yet. What is the positive way you can frame the elements that challenge you? An obstinate child may become a determined adult. An explosive child may grow into a passionate grown man or woman. A shy or cowed child can be guided into a thoughtful and empathetic adult.

Your own raw materials, the basic elements of your character, are also neither good nor bad on their own. Just as 'anger' is not a bad emotion, but inappropriately expressing it can be, your temperament is not objectively flawed or perfect. It simply is. Learn to pay attention to your natural reactions and make honest judgements about whether your responses are fair, appropriate, proportionate and reasonable. If not, practise developing the kind of self-discipline you would like to equip your child with in the future.

To love yourself, like yourself, respect yourself is key. You are a human being as complex as any other. You have a right to be here, just as you are. The right to be here does not extend to a right to impose yourself on other people without self-censorship. The experiences you have had up till now have shown you, more clearly than I can in mere words, the negative impact of an imposing, dominating and uncensored personality.

Nurture self-discipline as a natural way of being. The gifts of self-acceptance include knowing that not everyone will like you, and that is ok. As long as you can look back on your own behaviour without guilt, shame or regret, you are doing the best you can.

When you find those unpleasant feelings creep in, welcome them with open arms as you would welcome joy, peace and contentment. Just like the good feelings, bad feelings are only your navigator hard at work reminding you to return to your own guiding lights, reset your course and develop your artistry once more. Michelangelo once said he did not carve an angel out of stone, he saw the angel in the stone and set him free. You are the angel, and you can set yourself free.

Chapter 12

Don't stop me now!

How you do anything is how you do everything.
T Harv Eker

Today we close the circle. You have travelled a tremendous distance and achieved much of which you can be proud. Here you are, having journeyed through the badlands, working hard on developing those qualities I mentioned in the very first pages of this book — honesty, open-mindedness and a willingness to try something new. Your faith has been rewarded with evidence that by doing this, good things will indeed happen.

So Now What?

The circle becomes a spiral, an upward journey you can choose to keep climbing. Just after we close the circle with the question

Where am I now?,

it will shortly re-open again with the question

Who am I being today?

This lifelong journey is a way of living that opens you up to a deep spiritual experience of life. Not religious, but spiritual in the sense of being connected to something greater than yourself. The awareness of how interconnected we are cannot be escaped. How I am changes how I experience the world and, in turn, how the world responds to and experiences me.

But before you step onward along your path, called again to question who you are being day to day, let's sit for a moment at the threshold again and really examine where you are now.

When you began your journey, you were invited to think about leadership. What it means to you, how it is expressed by people around you, who you admire and aspire to be like. Today, turn that lens inward for a moment.

IN YOUR JOURNAL:
CELEBRATING THE JOURNEY

- What does assuming leadership of your family mean to you today?
- How are you expressing your leadership of your family right now?
- What do you want to acknowledge and celebrate about yourself today?
- What would you like to develop further?

Go back in your journal and look up the list of leadership qualities you identified. Back then I asked you to give yourself an honest score out of ten for each one.
- Can you do this again today?
- Has anything changed?
- Where have the improvements been?
- What still needs attention in order to develop?
- Can you celebrate your progress without berating yourself for being imperfect as well?

Soft Power

Women in leadership face many, many obstacles both in and out of the home. It's hard to take on roles that have traditionally been seen as masculine without questioning whether you will become masculine yourself. Our early explorations of leadership often involve challenging stereotypes and beliefs we hold about what taking charge of our lives might involve and how it will affect us

Learning about the different ways we can take charge of ourselves opens up a whole palette of colours with which to play. No longer is power associated with control, dominance, authority or ego. Power can be found in all the feminine archetypes history has to offer us too. The warrioress, the queen, the mother, the lover, the sorceress, the maiden, the crone… each one has a way of leading that is powerful, yet intrinsically feminine.

We call these female archetypes 'soft power' models. Soft power means leading from the parts of you that are feminine, both soft and strong, integrated with your whole self. Soft power is yielding, welcoming, inclusive, yet also wise, authoritative, commanding.

- Do you recognize one of these ways of being in yourself today?
- Do you feel called to step into a new archetype, or to step away from one you have inhabited for too long?

Perhaps the warrioress can stand down and the queen assume her throne. Maybe the maiden is able to dance again, playful, sensual and free. Or perhaps the mother, the giver and bringer of life, can settle into her powerful nurturing role with more ease. Enjoy the dance of each of these powerful aspects of your feminine power and allow yourself to welcome them all.

In truth, we each possess a balance of both masculine (active) and feminine (receptive) energy. The artistry that will soften your approach to leadership comes with learning to maintain this balance within yourself. As we are closing the circle, asking 'Where am I now?', our principle concern is one of balance. In moving away from a trial, or forward toward a goal, we necessarily call upon different aspects of our strength. Balance cannot be maintained perfectly, because to be always balanced we would also have to remain motionless.

We do not live suspended in space or seated on a lotus leaf. Certainly not with a wild tribe to run around after! So, the balance is observed in the macro picture, not the micro one. When you sketched your five or seven-year cycle of your life, you were able to trace the milestones and themes of your life in a macro lens. What fell above the line, what fell below?

You re-enter the cycle at the start of a new chunk of time, a new period of your life. While you reflect on this one just passing, give it the courtesy of expanding your view.

IN YOUR JOURNAL:
REFLECTING ON YOUR RECENT PAST

- In the five- or seven-year cycle you are in now, how will this period be recorded?
- Where will that balance appear?

> • What can you now write above the line as a gift, joy or benefit of the journey you've been on?
>
> Even in the darkest experiences, there will be something for which you can be grateful. You deserve to be happy. Your gratitude can be welcomed today without resentment.

At the start of this chapter I gave you a quote from a coach I admire very much. His name is T Harv Eker and he coined the phrase, 'How we do anything is how we do everything.' On my own journey, I listened to his work often and that phrase stayed with me.

I have chosen many mantras that have worked for me year on year.

The year I opened my business, I told myself over and over, 'A year from now, I'll be glad I did this today'. Through the late nights, the stumbles, the falls, the mess-ups, the realization I knew less than nothing about running a business, and even less than that about doing it with two tiny children in tow ... it kept me going. Somewhere along the way the mantra changed and became 'How I do anything is how I do everything'. So, anything I do, I do with dedication, self-belief and faith. The small things, the boring things, the tedious things. The things I would prefer to avoid or put off till tomorrow.

This mantra is shaping my character so, as we end our journey together in these pages, I offer it to you. Close your circle, and stand at the doorway to your next adventure, with the commitment that you will do any part of it with integrity in line with how you want all of your life to be reflected back to you.

Work with me

This journey is one of deep reflection and personal growth. It is no accident that when we go through meaningful rites of passage in life, these are traditionally witnessed by other people. Being witnessed, supported and celebrated as you transition from one stage of life into another is a very human desire. Witnesses help us to acknowledge momentous steps forward. They give depth of meaning to moments that should be recorded, remembered and rewarded.

I am your coach and also your witness. If you want to re-enter the cycle with me by your side, this is how you can work with me.

Family Vision, The One-To-One Journey

Apply today to walk through the whole of the vision-building journey with me by your side. We will meet once a week for an in-depth coaching call, exploring every step of the circle together. I will hold space for you to do the important and life-changing work of listening to yourself, claiming your personal values and learning to navigate by them no matter what life throws up in your way.

Together we will paint a picture of your life as you want it to be. I will hold the map, you will plot your course. You will climb your mountain with someone who has walked this path before, growing in confidence, experience and happiness with each step you take.

Places are limited to work with me one to one. Over the ten weeks we spend together you will feel your whole life perspective transformed in a fully supported space. I love working with women ready to make the change.

This is for you if you have been parenting alone and are ready to make a serious investment in your own happiness and the happiness of your children.

This path is for you if your relationship breakdown was defined by conflict, trauma, loss or abuse. If you found yourself in the pages of this book and know that a witness and travelling companion could transform your life, I'm waiting for your call. Find me at www.ninafarr.com

---

Abuse or conflict?

If you're not sure, take my quiz online at www. ninafarr.com to find out why your messy break-up

---

has left the whole family reeling. Knowing what you're dealing with is the first step to making it better.

The boundaries you need to set for yourself, your children and your ex will be different depending on whether you have been at war with each other and whether domestic abuse (emotional, psychological, financial, sexual or physical) has been present. It's not uncommon for victims of abuse to not recognize the signs at first.

Sadly, it's also far too common for couples who are angry to accuse each other of awful things, including abuse when none has actually occurred. Get perspective today so you can take the right path forward for your family, whatever it may be.

Family Vision, The Group Programme

Come on a journey with parents just like you, who are ready to make a change together. You can join from anywhere in the world, both men and women walk this path in community with each other.

The group programme is for you if you parent alone, or ever have done, and want to learn from parents just like you who are dedicated to bringing their best selves to family life.

The programme runs for eleven weeks. You can join at any time, beginning at the time that is right for you. This lively community of parents undertake the Family Vision journey together, benefitting from the stories, experiences and encouragement of each other along the way.

Every week you all have access to a group coaching call chaired via video conference by me personally, and you have access to the complete vault of resources created specifically for this programme. The Family Vision group programme is perfect if you are seeking your tribe, want to walk the path in good company or feel you want to journey the steps for a second, third or fourth time in company.

We are more than a group of current or historic single parents. We are a movement of modern families bringing a new wave of leadership, love and celebration to the world, reflecting the changing societies we live in, contributing to the positive development of a world we want to belong to. You are welcome to join whether you are a lone parent now, or were a lone parent for a time and are now blending your family with a new partner and children. Family is always changing — we are here for your own journey.

Masterclass

If you have been parenting alone for some time and are ready to integrate your learning and move with authority into the next phase of your life, Masterclass is for you.

Limited to small, single-sex, intimate groups, in Masterclass you will meet once a month for ten months across a calendar year. Every month, members are invited to bring the challenges, opportunities and issues that arise in their personal lone-parenting journeys.

Masterclass is a place to practise doing anything the way you want to do everything. You will learn to co-coach the members of your group to listen deeply to each other, to examine critically your own perspective and to lovingly challenge each other's limiting beliefs when they come up.

All the skills and attributes of the Family Vision journey you have developed in this book will be flexed and worked on in Masterclass. Not just in parenting, but in your personal relationships, your business or professional life, the way you manage your home, your health. We take a whole person approach that integrates everything you do with the principles most important to you. Nothing is 'off limits'. If it affects you and your family, you can bring it to Masterclass.

In Masterclass you will have the opportunity not only to work on yourself, you will step forward with a small group of dedicated peers, who will become a powerful network in your life as a lone parent. Masterclass is for you if you want to develop relationships that sustain you, challenge you and nurture you as someone who parents alone. It is the perfect place to develop the core skills of Chapter 11 so that you are able to use them with your children, your lovers, partners, friends and colleagues. Here, you will learn how to navigate a coaching cycle with confidence — even how to lead others along the path.

We meet at least once in person for a luxury weekend retreat to celebrate all that you are, and all you are becoming. Find out more at www.ninafarr.com

If our journey together ends here, let me take this moment now to thank you, celebrate you and honour you for the work you have done. I am privileged to have been a part of your unique and wonderful path as a parent.

To your happiness, and your success.

Nina Farr

About the author

Nina Farr is a Leadership Coach for lone parents, living in Exeter, Devon. When she isn't writing, speaking or coaching you will find her dipping her toes in the sea on Exmouth beach or wandering through the ancient woodlands of Devon with her family. A busy parent as well as professional, Nina is passionate about celebrating families in all their shapes and sizes.

Nina Farr is a Leadership Coach for lone parents, living in Exeter, Devon, UK. A coach, author and TEDx speaker, Nina has been a passionate advocate for families just like hers. Complicated, reworked and a little bit wonky. Mother to three, Nina loves children but know what hard work parenting can be. Especially when you throw in the complexities of a family that has or is changing shape.

Nina founded her coaching company as a lone parent, when her two oldest boys were two and nine-months. Writing her first business plan with the help of a select few single-mother friends, the idea to bring leadership skills to women everywhere who have experienced trauma, loss, grief, conflict and abuse was born. Nina has been sponsored on this journey by the

National Lottery, an international bank, social entrepreneurship grants and by Exeter University which has researched and evaluated her work.

An academic at heart, Nina is driven to create a legacy for women and children that is not only inspiring and heartfelt but also evidence based. She works in partnership with children's centres, schools, domestic-abuse agencies and most importantly women and children who have lived through the experience of family breakdown. Nina is a secret geek, not-so-secret beach bum and hippy mum to boot. When she's not speaking, coaching, writing and researching, you'll find her dipping her toes in the ocean on Exmouth beach or wandering through the ancient woodlands of Devon.